maranGraphics' Simplified Computer Guide

WordPerfect ®

VERSION 5.1

Richard Maran

maranGraphics Inc.
Mississauga, Ontario, Canada

maranGraphics' ™ *Simplified Computer Guide*
WordPerfect ® *Version 5.1*

Copyright ©   maranGraphics Inc. 1989
              5755 Coopers Avenue
              Mississauga, Ontario, Canada
              L4Z 1R9
              Phone: (416) 890-3300
              Fax: (416) 890-9434

Published 1990.   Second printing 1990
                  Third printing 1991
                  Fourth printing 1991
                  Fifth printing 1991
                  Sixth printing 1991

Canadian Cataloguing in Publication Data

Maran, Richard
    MaranGraphics' simplified computer guide
WordPerfect version 5.1

Originally published under title: WordPerfect training
and user guide.
Includes index.
ISBN 0-9695666-1-1

1. WordPerfect (Computer program).   2. Word
processing.   I. Title.   II. Title: WordPerfect version 5.1.
III. Title: WordPerfect training and user guide.

Z52.5.W65M37 1991.   652.5'5369   C92-093065-4

— — — — — — — — — — — — —

Acknowledgements

A special thanks to Mr. Keith Armstrong of the
Canadian Imperial Bank of Commerce for
proposing the overall concept and defining the
purpose of this guide. Also to Ms. Debbie
Johnston for her expert guidance on content and
consultation on technical accuracy.

To the dedicated staff at maranGraphics Inc.,
including Ed Corrado, Monica DeVries,
Lynne Hoppen, Jim C. Leung, Robert Maran,
Ruth Maran, Elizabeth Seeto, and Donna Williams
for the artwork development and technical
support.

And finally to Maxine Maran for providing the
organizational skill to keep the project under
control.

Trademark
Acknowledgement

WordPerfect is a
registered trademark of
WordPerfect
Corporation.

Cover Design:
Erich Volk

Production:
Monica DeVries
Jim C. Leung
Elizabeth Seeto

Linotronic L-300 Output:
HyperImage Inc.

— — — — — — — — — — — — —

Table of Contents

GLOBAL HELP

Press **F3** to access the Help screen displayed below.

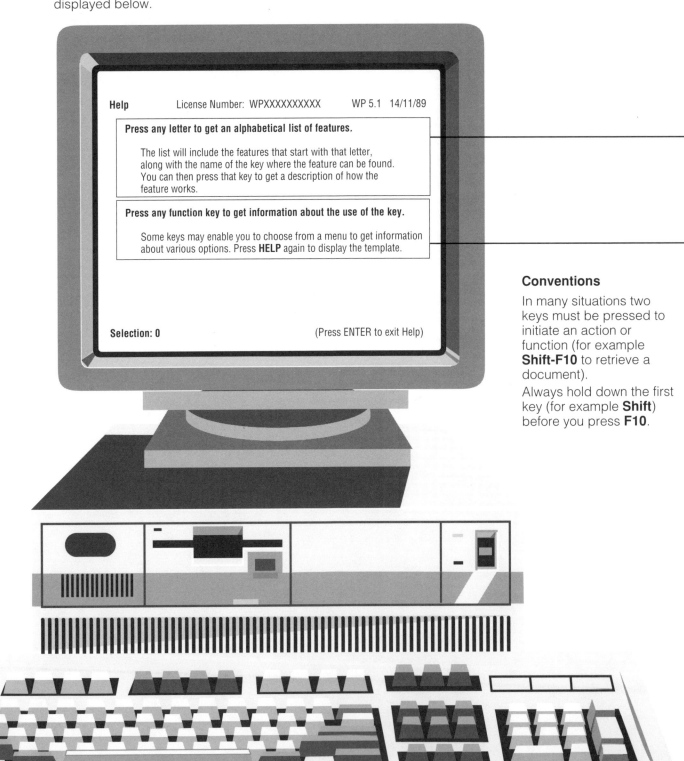

Help   License Number: WPXXXXXXXXXX   WP 5.1   14/11/89

Press any letter to get an alphabetical list of features.

The list will include the features that start with that letter, along with the name of the key where the feature can be found. You can then press that key to get a description of how the feature works.

Press any function key to get information about the use of the key.

Some keys may enable you to choose from a menu to get information about various options. Press **HELP** again to display the template.

Selection: 0   (Press ENTER to exit Help)

Conventions

In many situations two keys must be pressed to initiate an action or function (for example **Shift-F10** to retrieve a document).

Always hold down the first key (for example **Shift**) before you press **F10**.

GLOBAL
HELP

CONTEXT
SENSITIVE
HELP

HELP

PULL
DOWN
MENUS

CREATE
AND
EDIT A
DOCUMENT

MOVE, COPY,
DELETE, AND
RESTORE
TEXT

FORMAT
YOUR
DOCUMENTS

CHECK
YOUR
DOCUMENTS

PRINT
YOUR
DOCUMENTS

MANAGE
YOUR
DOCUMENTS

MERGE
YOUR
DOCUMENTS

Features	WordPerfect Key	Keystrokes
Backspace (Erase)	Backspace	Backspace
Backup Directory Location	Setup	Shft-F1,6
Backup Files, Automatic	Setup	Shft-F1,3,1,1
Backup Options	Setup	Shft-F1,3,1
Backward Search	<-Search	Shft-F2
Base Font	Font	Ctrl-F8,4
Base Font (Document)	Format	Shft-F8,3,3
Base Font (Printer)	Print	Shft-F7,s,3,5
Baseline Placement for Typesetters	Format	Shft-F8,4,6,5
Beep Options	Setup	Shft-F1,3,2
Binding Offset	Print	Shft-F7,b
Binding Offset (Default)	Setup	Shft-F1,4,8,1
Black and White, View Document In	Setup	Shft-F1,2,5,1
Block	Block	Alt-F4
Block, (Assign Variable w/Block On)	Macro Commands	Ctrl-PgUp
Block, Append (Block On)	Move	Ctrl-F4,1,4
Block, Center (Block On)	Center	Shft-F6
Block, Comment (Block On)	Text In/Out	Ctrl-F5
More... Press b to continue		

Selection: 0   (Press ENTER to exit Help)

List Features Alphabetically

You can list features by pressing the letter keys (**A** to **Z**). For example to list features starting with B, press **B**.

Block On/Off

Defines a block of text on which various operations may be performed. The block will be highlighted as it is defined.

To define a block:

1. Position the cursor at the beginning or end of the block of text.
2. Press **Block** (Alt-F4).
3. Move the cursor to the opposite end of the block. Use the arrow keys, or type a character to advance to that character. You can also use ->Search or <-Search to move the highlighting to the character(s) entered here.

You may then use the following features:
- **Append** - Press Move to append the block to the end of a file.
- **Bold** - Embolden the highlighted text.
- **Comment** - Press Text In/Out to change text to a comment.
- Underline - Underline text.
- Center - Center blocked lines.
- **Delete** - Press Del or Backspace to delete the block.
- Flush Rgt - Move blocked lines to the right margin.
- Font - Change the appearance or size of printed text.
- **Type 1 for more ...**

Selection: 0   (Press ENTER to exit Help)

Display Function Key Explanations

You can display explanations on any function key by pressing it. For example press **Alt-F4** (The Block Command).

WordPerfect 5.1 Template (IBM Layout)

F1	**Shell** SETUP Thesaurus —Cancel—	**Spell** <-SEARCH Replace Search->	F2
F3	**Screen** SWITCH Reveal Codes —Help—	**Move** ->INDENT<- Block ->Indent	F4
F5	**Text In/Out** DATE/OUTLINE Mark Text —List—	**Tab Align** CENTRE Flush Right —Bold—	F6
F7	**Footnote** PRINT Columns/Table —Exit—	**Font** FORMAT Style Underline	F8
F9	**Merge/Sort** MERGE CODES Graphics End Field	**Macro Define** RETRIEVE Macro Save	F10

Legend:

Ctrl + Function Key
SHIFT + FUNCTION KEY
Alt + Function Key
Function Key alone

Selection: 0   (Press ENTER to exit Help)

Display Command Template

Press **F3** again.

To exit help
Press **Enter**.

CONTEXT SENSITIVE HELP

After typing a command such as **Save** (F7), **Search** (F2) or **Replace** (Alt-F2), you may want help on that specific command.

To exit help
Press **Enter**.

SAVE (F7) WITH HELP (F3)

December 20, 1989

Subject: WordPerfect Training Program

To: Tom Smith

We have developed a new training method for teaching word processing software. It uses integrated text and graphics to present concepts that are extremely difficult to explain with text alone. Each topic is presented as a graphic. The copy is then annotated into the graphic to make all elements on the page context sensitive.

I am looking forward to showing you how the process works at our meeting this coming Friday.

Lynne Hoppen

Save document? Yes (No)

Exit

Gives you the option to save your document and then allows you to either exit WordPerfect or clear the screen.

Exit is also used to exit from editing headers, styles, footnotes, etc.

When you are in screens other than editing screens, pressing Exit leaves menus and will normally return you to the normal editing screen (you may need to press Exit more than once).

Selection: 0   (Press ENTER to exit Help)

---

❶ Press **F7** to save the document.

❷ Press **F3** for Help.

Note: The document above is shown as an example. Any document you create would apply.

● A context sensitive Help screen appears.

GLOBAL
HELP

CONTEXT
SENSITIVE
HELP

HELP

SEARCH (F2) WITH HELP (F3)

```
December 20, 1989

Subject:  WordPerfect Training Program

To:  Tom Smith

We have developed a new training method for teaching word
processing software. It uses integrated text and graphics to
present concepts that are extremely difficult to explain with text
alone. Each topic is presented as a graphic. The copy is then
annotated into the graphic to make all elements on the page
context sensitive.

I am looking forward to showing you how the process works at
our meeting this coming Friday.

Lynne Hoppen

->Srch:
```

```
Search

    Searches forward (F2) or backward (Shift-F2) through your
    text for a specific combination of characters and/or codes.
    After entering the search text, press Search again to start the
    search. If the text is found, the cursor will be positioned just
    after (to the right of) it. Lowercase letters in the search text
    match both lowercase and uppercase. Uppercase letters
    match only uppercase.

    Extended Search
    Pressing Home before pressing Search extends the search
    into headers, footers, footnotes, endnotes, graphics box
    captions, and text boxes. To continue the extended search,
    press Home, Search.

Selection: 0                          (Press ENTER to exit Help)
```

❶ Press **F2** to search for a word, phrase or sentence.　❷ Press **F3** for Help.　● A context sensitive Help screen appears.

REPLACE (ALT-F2) WITH HELP (F3)

```
December 20, 1989

Subject:  WordPerfect Training Program

To:  Tom Smith

We have developed a new training method for teaching word
processing software. It uses integrated text and graphics to
present concepts that are extremely difficult to explain with text
alone. Each topic is presented as a graphic. The copy is then
annotated into the graphic to make all elements on the page
context sensitive.

I am looking forward to showing you how the process works at
our meeting this coming Friday.

Lynne Hoppen

w/Confirm? No (Yes)
```

```
Replace

Helps you replace every occurrence of a word, phrase, or WordPerfect
code with another word, phrase or code. All occurrences can be
replaced or, with the Confirm option on, you can answer yes or no to
each replacement.

After you press Replace, the following prompts will appear:

    w/Confirm?:  Type y to confirm each replacement, type n to have
                 all replacements made without confirmation.
       -> Srch:  Enter the old text and/or codes to be replaced and
                 press Search.
  Replace with:  Enter the replacement text and/or codes and
                 press Search again.

Selection: 0                          (Press ENTER to exit Help)
```

❶ Press **Alt-F2** to replace a word, phrase or sentence with another word, phrase or sentence.　❷ Press **F3** for Help.　● A context sensitive Help screen appears.

PULL
DOWN
MENUS

CREATE
AND
EDIT A
DOCUMENT

MOVE, COPY,
DELETE, AND
RESTORE
TEXT

FORMAT
YOUR
DOCUMENTS

CHECK
YOUR
DOCUMENTS

PRINT
YOUR
DOCUMENTS

MANAGE
YOUR
DOCUMENTS

MERGE
YOUR
DOCUMENTS

Pull Down menus allow you to select a command without having to remember function key names such as Search (F2) or Spellcheck (Ctrl-F2)

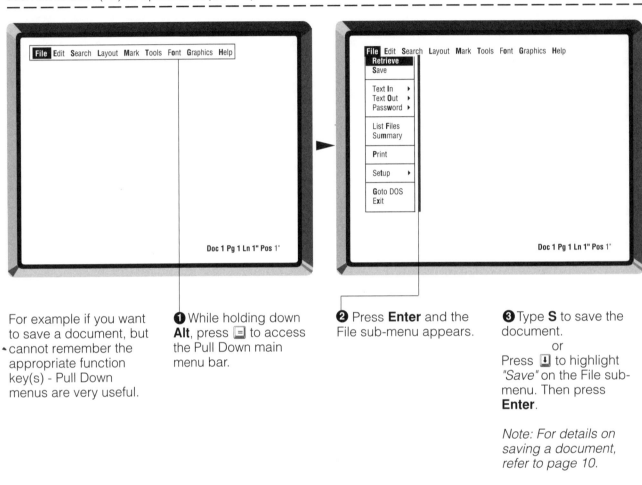

For example if you want to save a document, but cannot remember the appropriate function key(s) - Pull Down menus are very useful.

❶ While holding down **Alt**, press ▣ to access the Pull Down main menu bar.

❷ Press **Enter** and the File sub-menu appears.

❸ Type **S** to save the document.
or
Press ▣ to highlight *"Save"* on the File sub-menu. Then press **Enter**.

Note: For details on saving a document, refer to page 10.

To exit pull down menus
Press **F1** enough times to return to the typing screen.

HELP

PULL
DOWN
MENUS

CREATE
AND
LIST A
DOCUMENTT

MOVE, COPY,
DELETE, AND
RESTORE
TEXT

FORMAT
YOUR
DOCUMENTS

CHECK
YOUR
DOCUMENTS

PRINT
YOUR
DOCUMENTS

MANAGE
YOUR
DOCUMENTS

MERGE
YOUR
DOCUMENTS

● To move back and forth along the main menu, press **Enter** and then ▣ or ▣.

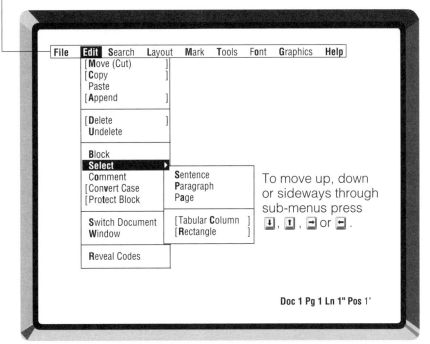

To move up, down or sideways through sub-menus press ▣, ▣, ▣ or ▣.

Doc 1 Pg 1 Ln 1" Pos 1"

● To select a command:
– Type the bold letter in the command.
or
– Press ▣ until the command is highlighted. Then press **Enter**.

The ▶ marker beside a command indicates that another sub-menu is available under that command.

7

START A DOCUMENT

After you start WordPerfect a blank screen appears.

Begin entering text. Notice that WordPerfect automatically moves the cursor to the next line as you type. This is called *word wrap*.

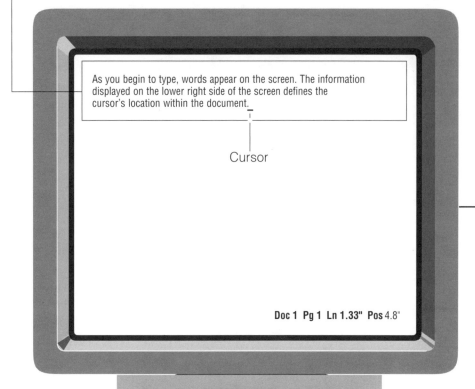

As you begin to type, words appear on the screen. The information displayed on the lower right side of the screen defines the cursor's location within the document.

Cursor

Doc 1 Pg 1 Ln 1.33" Pos 4.8"

Margins, line spacing and type style are already preset for you. Later in this guide you will be shown how to modify these preset values.

HELP

PULL DOWN MENUS

CREATE AND EDIT A DOCUMENT

MOVE, COPY, DELETE, AND RESTORE TEXT

FORMAT YOUR DOCUMENTS

CHECK YOUR DOCUMENTS

PRINT YOUR DOCUMENTS

MANAGE YOUR DOCUMENTS

MERGE YOUR DOCUMENTS

Adding a space between paragraphs

After reaching the end of the first paragraph press **Enter**. The cursor moves to the next line.

Press **Enter** again to make the cursor move down another line. Then start typing the second paragraph.

As you begin to type, words appear on the screen. The information displayed on the lower right side of the screen defines the cursor's location within the document.

Electronic word processing offers productivity improvements and the ability to visually enhance the documents you create.

| Doc 1 | Pg 1 | Ln 1.83" | Pos 6.7" |

Status Line

The cursor's location within the document is defined with these four coordinates.

Doc 1
WordPerfect allows you to work on two documents simultaneously. Doc 1 is currently displayed on the screen.

Pg 1
This identifies which page the cursor is currently on.

Ln 1.83"
This defines how far (in inches) the cursor is from the top of the page.

Pos 6.7"
This defines how far (in inches) the cursor is from the left side of the page.

SAVE AND NAME A DOCUMENT

SAVE AND NAME A DOCUMENT

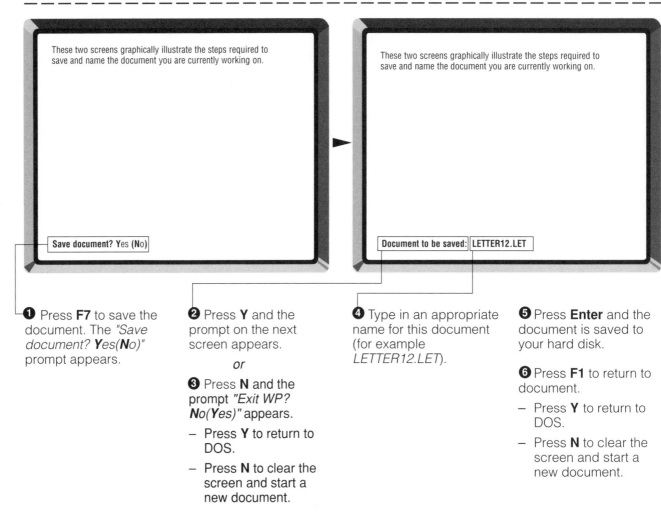

These two screens graphically illustrate the steps required to save and name the document you are currently working on.

These two screens graphically illustrate the steps required to save and name the document you are currently working on.

Save document? Yes (No)

Document to be saved: LETTER12.LET

❶ Press **F7** to save the document. The *"Save document? Yes(No)"* prompt appears.

❷ Press **Y** and the prompt on the next screen appears.

or

❸ Press **N** and the prompt *"Exit WP? No(Yes)"* appears.
  – Press **Y** to return to DOS.
  – Press **N** to clear the screen and start a new document.

❹ Type in an appropriate name for this document (for example *LETTER12.LET*).

❺ Press **Enter** and the document is saved to your hard disk.

❻ Press **F1** to return to document.
  – Press **Y** to return to DOS.
  – Press **N** to clear the screen and start a new document.

Save a document and have it remain on screen

Press **F10** and the screen prompt *"document to be saved:"* appears. Type in the name of your document and press **Enter**. The document is saved to your hard disk and still appears on screen.

Naming your document

ABCDE123 . EXT

● This part of the name can contain up to 8 characters.

● This part of the name can contain up to 3 characters or be omitted.

The following characters are allowed:

● The letters A to Z, upper or lower case
● The digits 0 through 9
● $ # & @ ! % () - [] and _

START A
DOCUMENT

**SAVE AND
NAME A
DOCUMENT**

RETRIEVE
DOCUMENT

CURSOR
CONTROL

INSERT OR
TYPEOVER
TEXT

DELETE
TEXT

DISPLAY
AND USE
DOC 1 AND
DOC 2

Directory Organization

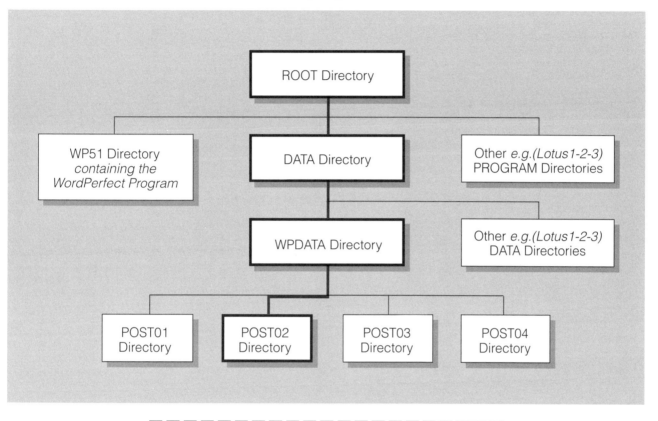

The path from the *ROOT Directory* to the *POST02 Directory* is:

C:\DATA\WPDATA\POST02

Create a new directory

❶ Press **F5**.

❷ Press ▣ to create a new directory.

❸ Type in the name of the new directory (for example **C:\DATA\WPDATA\POST05**) and press **Enter**.

❹ After the prompt *"Create C:\DATA\WPDATA\POST05? **N**o (**Yes**)"* appears, press **Y**.

Change the current directory

❶ Press **F5**.

❷ Press ▣ to change the current directory.

❸ Type in the directory you want to change to (for example **C:\DATA\WPDATA\POST05**) and press **Enter** twice.

❹ Press **F1** to clear screen.

HELP

PULL
DOWN
MENUS

**CREATE
AND
EDIT A
DOCUMENT**

MOVE, COPY,
DELETE, AND
RESTORE
TEXT

FORMAT
YOUR
DOCUMENTS

CHECK
YOUR
DOCUMENTS

PRINT
YOUR
DOCUMENTS

MANAGE
YOUR
DOCUMENTS

MERGE
YOUR
DOCUMENTS

RETRIEVE
DOCUMENT

RETRIEVE DOCUMENT *(for document names you remember)*

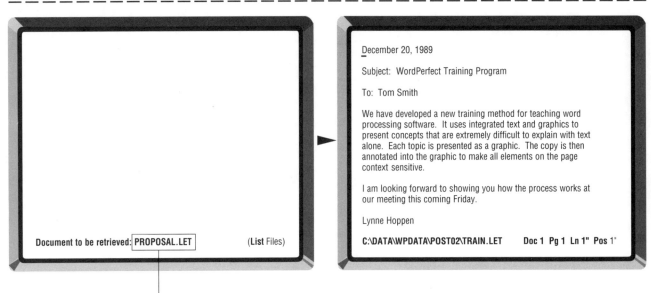

Document to be retrieved: **PROPOSAL.LET**   (**List** Files)

December 20, 1989

Subject: WordPerfect Training Program

To: Tom Smith

We have developed a new training method for teaching word processing software. It uses integrated text and graphics to present concepts that are extremely difficult to explain with text alone. Each topic is presented as a graphic. The copy is then annotated into the graphic to make all elements on the page context sensitive.

I am looking forward to showing you how the process works at our meeting this coming Friday.

Lynne Hoppen

C:\DATA\WPDATA\POST02\TRAIN.LET   Doc 1 Pg 1 Ln 1" Pos 1"

For document in the current directory

❶ Press **Shift-F10**.

❷ Type in the file name (for example: PROPOSAL.LET).

❸ Press **Enter**.

For documents not in the current directory

❶ Press **Shift-F10**.

❷ Type in the new directory and file name (for example: C:\DATA\WPDATA\POST02\ TRAIN.LET).

❸ Press **Enter**.

● The retrieved document is displayed.

● This message appears if:

– The document's name was typed incorrectly.

– The name of the document typed does not exist in the current directory.

ERROR: File not found--PROPSAL.LET

To cancel the retrieve or list documents command
Press **F1**.

START A
DOCUMENT

SAVE AND
NAME A
DOCUMENT

**RETRIEVE
DOCUMENT**

CURSOR
CONTROL

INSERT OR
TYPEOVER
TEXT

DELETE
TEXT

DISPLAY
AND USE
DOC 1 AND
DOC 2

HELP

PULL
DOWN
MENUS

**CREATE
AND
EDIT A
DOCUMENT**

MOVE, COPY,
DELETE, AND
RESTORE
TEXT

FORMAT
YOUR
DOCUMENTS

CHECK
YOUR
DOCUMENTS

PRINT
YOUR
DOCUMENTS

MANAGE
YOUR
DOCUMENTS

MERGE
YOUR
DOCUMENTS

LIST AND RETRIEVE DOCUMENTS *(for document names you cannot remember)*

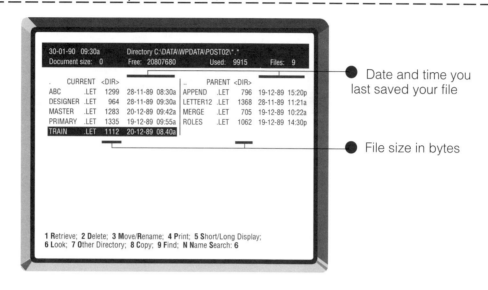

● Date and time you last saved your file

● File size in bytes

Retrieve Documents

❶ Before retrieving a document, press **F7** and then **N** twice to clear the screen.

❷ Press **F5**.

❸ Be sure the directory shown is correct. If not, follow the steps on page 11 to change directories. If you are in the correct directory, press **F5** again.

❹ Use the cursor keys to highlight the document you want to retrieve.

❺ Press **1** to retrieve the selected document.

The Heading

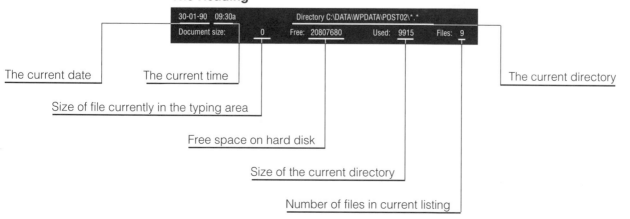

The current date

The current time

Size of file currently in the typing area

Free space on hard disk

Size of the current directory

Number of files in current listing

The current directory

13

CURSOR CONTROL

WordPerfect features a wide range of cursor control operations to help you navigate within your document.

Press this key to move the cursor one line up.

WordPerfect features a wide range of cursor control operations to help you navigate within your document.

Press this key to move the cursor one line down.

WordPerfect features a wide range of cursor control operations to help you navigate within your document.

Press this key to move the cursor left by one character.

WordPerfect features a wide range of cursor control operations to help you navigate within your document.

Press this key to move the cursor right by one character.

WordPerfect features a wide range of cursor control operations to help you navigate within your document.

Ctrl Press these keys to move the cursor to the next word.

WordPerfect features a wide range of cursor control operations to help you navigate within your document.

Ctrl Press these keys to move the cursor to the previous word.

START A
DOCUMENT

SAVE AND
NAME A
DOCUMENT

RETRIEVE
DOCUMENT

**CURSOR
CONTROL**

INSERT OR
TYPEOVER
TEXT

DELETE
TEXT

DISPLAY
AND USE
DOC 1 AND
DOC 2

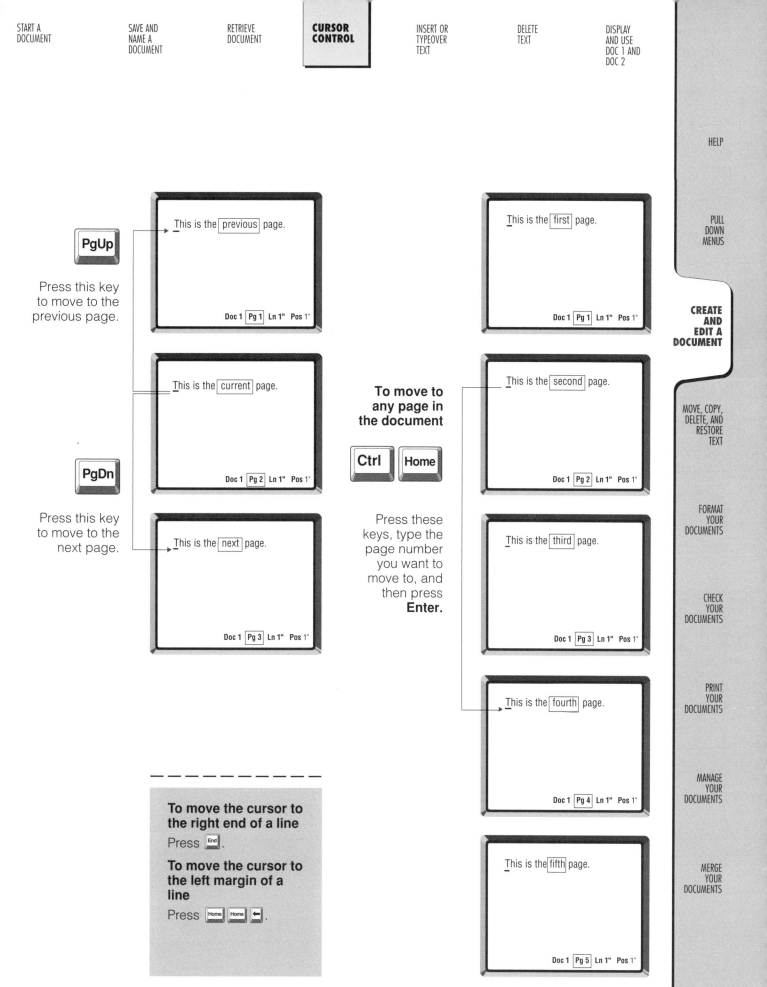

PgUp

Press this key
to move to the
previous page.

PgDn

Press this key
to move to the
next page.

This is the previous page.

Doc 1 | Pg 1 | Ln 1" Pos 1"

This is the current page.

Doc 1 | Pg 2 | Ln 1" Pos 1"

This is the next page.

Doc 1 | Pg 3 | Ln 1" Pos 1"

**To move to
any page in
the document**

Ctrl **Home**

Press these
keys, type the
page number
you want to
move to, and
then press
Enter.

This is the first page.

Doc 1 | Pg 1 | Ln 1" Pos 1"

This is the second page.

Doc 1 | Pg 2 | Ln 1" Pos 1"

This is the third page.

Doc 1 | Pg 3 | Ln 1" Pos 1"

This is the fourth page.

Doc 1 | Pg 4 | Ln 1" Pos 1"

This is the fifth page.

Doc 1 | Pg 5 | Ln 1" Pos 1"

**To move the cursor to
the right end of a line**
Press [End].

**To move the cursor to
the left margin of a
line**
Press [Home] [Home] [←].

HELP

PULL
DOWN
MENUS

**CREATE
AND
EDIT A
DOCUMENT**

MOVE, COPY,
DELETE, AND
RESTORE
TEXT

FORMAT
YOUR
DOCUMENTS

CHECK
YOUR
DOCUMENTS

PRINT
YOUR
DOCUMENTS

MANAGE
YOUR
DOCUMENTS

MERGE
YOUR
DOCUMENTS

INSERT OR TYPEOVER TEXT

INSERT TEXT

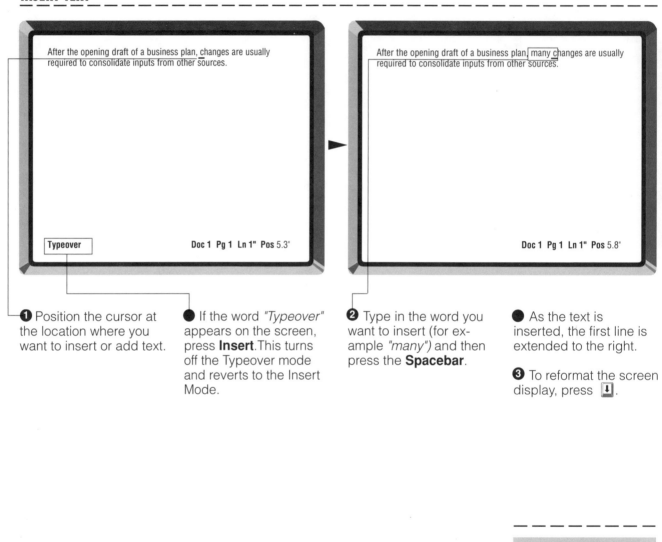

After the opening draft of a business plan, changes are usually required to consolidate inputs from other sources.

Typeover

Doc 1 Pg 1 Ln 1" Pos 5.3"

After the opening draft of a business plan, many changes are usually required to consolidate inputs from other sources.

Doc 1 Pg 1 Ln 1" Pos 5.8"

1 Position the cursor at the location where you want to insert or add text.

● If the word *"Typeover"* appears on the screen, press **Insert**.This turns off the Typeover mode and reverts to the Insert Mode.

2 Type in the word you want to insert (for example *"many"*) and then press the **Spacebar**.

● As the text is inserted, the first line is extended to the right.

3 To reformat the screen display, press ⬇.

Insert blank spaces

Blank spaces can be inserted anywhere in text by pressing the **Spacebar**.

This feature only applies to the Insert mode.

START A
DOCUMENT

SAVE AND
NAME A
DOCUMENT

RETRIEVE
DOCUMENT

CURSOR
CONTROL

**INSERT OR
TYPEOVER
TEXT**

DELETE
TEXT

DISPLAY
AND USE
DOC 1 AND
DOC 2

HELP

PULL
DOWN
MENUS

**CREATE
AND
EDIT A
DOCUMENT**

MOVE, COPY,
DELETE, AND
RESTORE
TEXT

FORMAT
YOUR
DOCUMENTS

CHECK
YOUR
DOCUMENTS

PRINT
YOUR
DOCUMENTS

MANAGE
YOUR
DOCUMENTS

MERGE
YOUR
DOCUMENTS

TYPEOVER TEXT

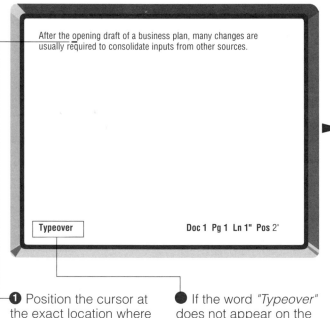

After the opening draft of a business plan, many changes are usually required to consolidate inputs from other sources.

Typeover   Doc 1 Pg 1 Ln 1" Pos 2"

After the initial draft of a business plan, many changes are usually required to consolidate inputs from other sources.

Typeover   Doc 1 Pg 1 Ln 1" Pos 2.7"

❶ Position the cursor at the exact location where you want to typeover or replace text.

● If the word *"Typeover"* does not appear on the screen, press **Insert** to turn on the Typeover Mode.

❷ Typeover the existing text (for example replace *"opening"* with *"initial"*).

❸ Press **Insert** to turn off the Typeover Mode.

*Note: If the Typeover word is shorter than the word it replaces, press **Delete** to remove the unwanted characters.*

*If the typeover word is longer than the word it replaces, move the word following it over with the **Spacebar** before starting the Typeover mode.*

Insert blank lines

Blank lines can be inserted anywhere in the document by pressing **Enter**.

This feature applies to both the Insert and Typeover modes.

DELETE
TEXT

DELETE CHARACTERS

Subject: New Training Program

Educators stress the importance of links between pieces of information in the memory retention process|s| .

Our new training program links discreet pieces of information through a comprehensive visual sorting, connecting and grouping process called Hypergraphics.

Doc 1 Pg 1 Ln 1.5" Pos 5.3"

Delete characters at the cursor

❶ Move the cursor to the character you want to delete (for example the extra *"s"* in the word process).

❷ Press **Delete** to delete the extra *"s"*.

Delete characters to the left of the cursor

❶ Move the cursor to the right of the character you want to delete.

❷ Press **Backspace**.

DELETE WORDS

Subject: New Training Program

Educators stress the importance of links between pieces of information in the memory retention process.

Our new training program links discreet pieces of information through a comprehensive |visual| sorting, connecting and grouping process called Hypergraphics.

Doc 1 Pg 1 Ln 2" Pos 3.5"

Delete the word at the cursor

❶ Move the cursor to any position in the word that you want deleted .

❷ Press **Ctrl-Backspace** to delete *"visual"*.

The three most recent deletions can be recovered, as long as you have not left WordPerfect.

Restored text will be placed wherever the cursor is positioned at the time of the restore.

To restore the most recent text deletion

Press **F1** to display the most recent text deletion.

Press **1** to restore the displayed text.

START A
DOCUMENT

SAVE AND
NAME A
DOCUMENT

RETRIEVE
DOCUMENT

CURSOR
CONTROL

INSERT OR
TYPEOVER
TEXT

**DELETE
TEXT**

DISPLAY
AND USE
DOC 1 AND
DOC 2

HELP

PULL
DOWN
MENUS

**CREATE
AND
EDIT A
DOCUMENT**

MOVE, COPY,
DELETE, AND
RESTORE
TEXT

FORMAT
YOUR
DOCUMENTS

CHECK
YOUR
DOCUMENTS

PRINT
YOUR
DOCUMENTS

MANAGE
YOUR
DOCUMENTS

MERGE
YOUR
DOCUMENTS

DELETE LINES

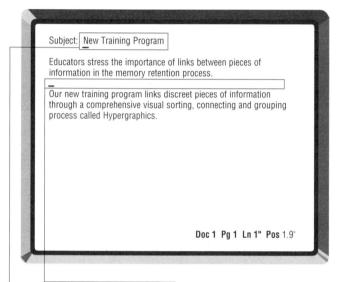

DELETE PAGES

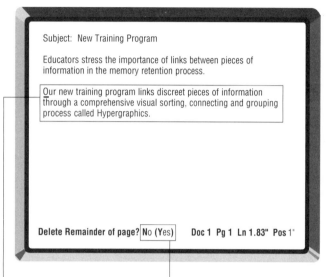

Delete the remainder of the line from the cursor position

❶ To delete all or part of a line, move the cursor to where you want the deletion to start from.

❷ Press **Ctrl-End** and *"New Training Program"* is deleted.

Delete a blank line

❶ Move the cursor to the blank line you want to delete.

❷ Press **Delete** and the paragraph starting with *"Our new training..."* moves up 1 line.

Delete the remainder of the page from the cursor

❶ To delete all or part of a page, move the cursor to where you want the deletion to start from.

❷ Press **Ctrl-PgDn**. The screen prompt: *"Delete Remainder of page? No (Yes)"* appears.

❸ Press**:**

N – To cancel the command

Y – To delete the remainder of the page

If you press **Y**, all text from the cursor to the bottom of the page is deleted.

To restore the second text deletion

Press **F1** and then press **2** to display the second text deletion.

Press **1** to restore the displayed text.

To restore the third text deletion

Press **F1** and then press **2** twice to display the third text deletion.

Press **1** to restore the displayed text.

19

Each document in WordPerfect contains 2 Windows. The Windows are called Doc 1 and Doc 2.

This feature is very useful for copying or moving text between documents.

DOC 1 WINDOW

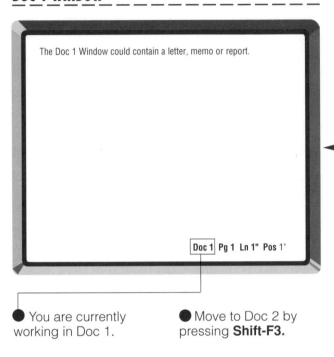

The Doc 1 Window could contain a letter, memo or report.

Doc 1 Pg 1 Ln 1" Pos 1"

● You are currently working in Doc 1.

● Move to Doc 2 by pressing **Shift-F3.**

DISPLAYING DOC 1 AND DOC 2 TOGETHER

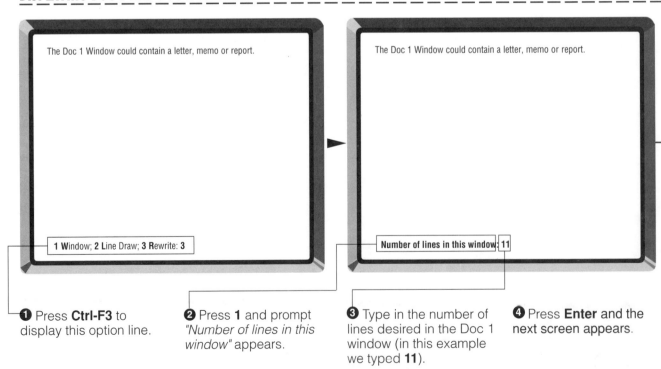

The Doc 1 Window could contain a letter, memo or report.

1 Window; 2 Line Draw; 3 Rewrite: 3

The Doc 1 Window could contain a letter, memo or report.

Number of lines in this window: 11

❶ Press **Ctrl-F3** to display this option line.

❷ Press **1** and prompt *"Number of lines in this window"* appears.

❸ Type in the number of lines desired in the Doc 1 window (in this example we typed **11**).

❹ Press **Enter** and the next screen appears.

START A
DOCUMENT

SAVE AND
NAME A
DOCUMENT

RETRIEVE
DOCUMENT

CURSOR
CONTROL

INSERT OR
TYPEOVER
TEXT

DELETE
TEXT

**DISPLAY
AND USE
DOC 1 AND
DOC 2**

HELP

PULL
DOWN
MENUS

**CREATE
AND
EDIT A
DOCUMENT**

MOVE, COPY,
DELETE, AND
RESTORE
TEXT

FORMAT
YOUR
DOCUMENTS

CHECK
YOUR
DOCUMENTS

PRINT
YOUR
DOCUMENTS

MANAGE
YOUR
DOCUMENTS

MERGE
YOUR
DOCUMENTS

DOC 2 WINDOW

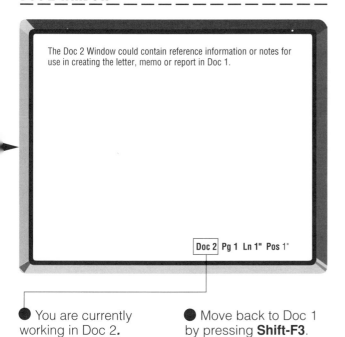

The Doc 2 Window could contain reference information or notes for use in creating the letter, memo or report in Doc 1.

Doc 2 Pg 1 Ln 1" Pos 1"

● You are currently working in Doc 2.

● Move back to Doc 1 by pressing **Shift-F3**.

The Doc 1 Window could contain a letter, memo or report.

Doc 1 Pg 1 Ln 1" Pos 1"

The Doc 2 Window could contain reference information or notes for use in creating the letter, memo or report in Doc 1.

Doc 2 Pg 1 Ln 1" Pos 1"

To restore the active window to full screen size

❶ Press **Ctrl-F3**.

❷ Select the window option by pressing **1**.

❸ Type 24 and press **Enter**.

● The direction of the arrows in the middle ruler line indicates which window is active.

● Press **Shift-F3** to move between Doc 1 and Doc 2 windows.

▲▲▲▲▲ Indicates top window active

▼▼▼▼▼ Indicates bottom window active

21

SELECT TEXT

Before you can copy, move or delete text, you must select it by using either of the two methods described on the next page.

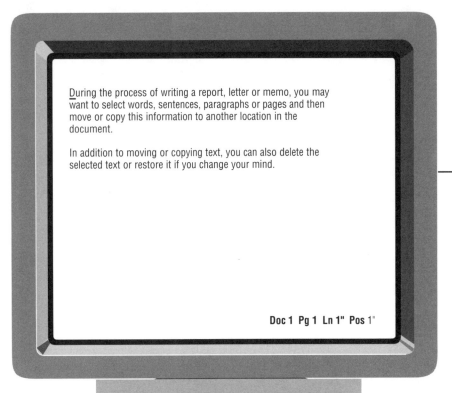

During the process of writing a report, letter or memo, you may want to select words, sentences, paragraphs or pages and then move or copy this information to another location in the document.

In addition to moving or copying text, you can also delete the selected text or restore it if you change your mind.

Doc 1 Pg 1 Ln 1" Pos 1"

SELECT
TEXT

MOVE
AND COPY
TEXT

DELETE AND
RESTORE
TEXT

HELP

PULL
DOWN
MENUS

CREATE
AND
EDIT A
DOCUMENT

MOVE, COPY,
DELETE, AND
RESTORE
TEXT

FORMAT
YOUR
DOCUMENTS

CHECK
YOUR
DOCUMENTS

PRINT
YOUR
DOCUMENTS

MANAGE
YOUR
DOCUMENTS

MERGE
YOUR
DOCUMENTS

SELECT A TEXT BLOCK

This method allows you to select any continuous group of characters, words, sentences or pages.

Note: A text block is defined as a selected group of characters.

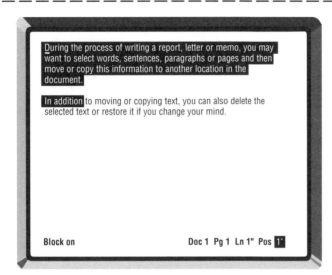

Block on   Doc 1 Pg 1 Ln 1" Pos 1"

❶ Position the cursor at the first character of the text block you want to select.

Press **F12** (or **Alt-F4**). This initiates the selection of a text block.

Select the text block with the cursor control keys.

As you move the cursor the text is highlighted.

To cancel
Press **F1**.

SELECT A SENTENCE, PARAGRAPH OR PAGE

This method allows you to select a whole sentence, paragraph or page without using the cursor control keys.

During the process of writing a report, letter or memo, you may want to select words, sentences, paragraphs or pages and then move or copy this information to another location in the document.

In addition to moving or copying text, you can also delete the selected text or restore it if you change your mind.

Move: 1 Sentence; **2** Paragraph; **3** Page; Retrieve : **0**

❶ Position the cursor anywhere in the sentence, paragraph or page you want to select.

❷ Press **Ctrl-F4**. The Move menu appears.

❸ Press:

1 to select a sentence
2 to select a paragraph
3 to select a whole page

In this example we pressed **1**.

To cancel
Press **F1**.

23

MOVE AND COPY TEXT

SELECT A TEXT BLOCK

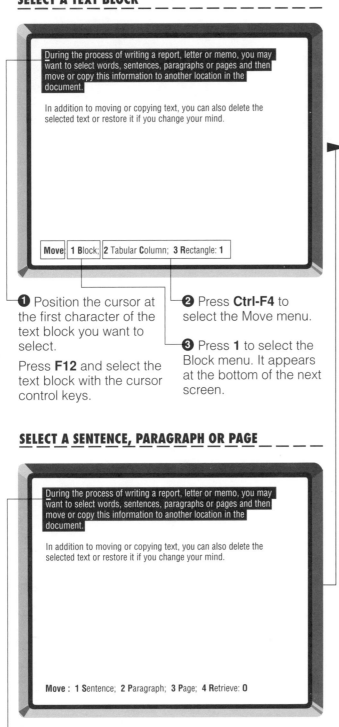

During the process of writing a report, letter or memo, you may want to select words, sentences, paragraphs or pages and then move or copy this information to another location in the document.

In addition to moving or copying text, you can also delete the selected text or restore it if you change your mind.

Move | **1 B**lock; | **2 T**abular **C**olumn; **3 R**ectangle: **1**

❶ Position the cursor at the first character of the text block you want to select.

Press **F12** and select the text block with the cursor control keys.

❷ Press **Ctrl-F4** to select the Move menu.

❸ Press **1** to select the Block menu. It appears at the bottom of the next screen.

During the process of writing a report, letter or memo, you may want to select words, sentences, paragraphs or pages and then move or copy this information to another location in the document.

In addition to moving or copying text, you can also delete the selected text or restore it if you change your mind.

1 Move; | **2 C**opy; **3 D**elete; **4 A**ppend: **0**

Ⓐ To move the selected text, press **1**.

Ⓑ To copy the selected text, press **2**.

SELECT A SENTENCE, PARAGRAPH OR PAGE

During the process of writing a report, letter or memo, you may want to select words, sentences, paragraphs or pages and then move or copy this information to another location in the document.

In addition to moving or copying text, you can also delete the selected text or restore it if you change your mind.

Move : **1 S**entence; **2 P**aragraph; **3 P**age; **4 R**etrieve: **0**

❶ Position the cursor anywhere in the sentence, paragraph or page you want to select.

❷ Press **Ctrl-F4** and then press **1**, **2**, or **3**. The Block menu at the bottom of the next screen appears.

To cancel a move/copy operation

Press **F1**.

24

SELECT
TEXT

**MOVE
AND COPY
TEXT**

DELETE AND
RESTORE
TEXT

HELP

PULL
DOWN
MENUS

CREATE
AND
EDIT A
DOCUMENT

**MOVE, COPY,
DELETE, AND
RESTORE
TEXT**

FORMAT
YOUR
DOCUMENTS

CHECK
YOUR
DOCUMENTS

PRINT
YOUR
DOCUMENTS

MANAGE
YOUR
DOCUMENTS

MERGE
YOUR
DOCUMENTS

MOVE SELECTED TEXT

In addition to moving or copying text, you can also delete the selected text or restore it if you change your mind.[_]

Move cursor; press **Enter** to retrieve.

In addition to moving or copying text, you can also delete the selected text or restore it if you change your mind.

During the process of writing a report, letter or memo, you may want to select words, sentences, paragraphs or pages and then move or copy this information to another location in the document.

Doc 1 Pg 1 Ln 1.67" Pos 1"

❹ Position the cursor at the location you want the selected text moved to.

Note:The selected text is deleted from the screen.

❺ Press **Enter** to paste the selected text into its new location.

❻ Press **Enter** twice to move the selected text down 2 lines.

COPY SELECTED TEXT

During the process of writing a report, letter or memo, you may want to select words, sentences, paragraphs or pages and then move or copy this information to another location in the document.

In addition to moving or copying text, you can also delete the selected text or restore it if you change your mind.[_]

Move cursor; press **Enter** to retrieve.

During the process of writing a report, letter or memo, you may want to select words, sentences, paragraphs or pages and then move or copy this information to another location in the document.

In addition to moving or copying text, you can also delete the selected text or restore it if you change your mind.

During the process of writing a report, letter or memo, you may want to select words, sentences, paragraphs or pages and then move or copy this information to another location in the document.

Doc 1 Pg 1 Ln 2.33" Pos 1"

❸ Position the cursor at the location you want the selected text copied to.

Note:The selected text is not deleted from the screen.

❹ Press **Enter** to paste the selected text into its new location.

❺ Press **Enter** twice to move the selected text down 2 lines.

DELETE AND RESTORE TEXT

DELETE A TEXT BLOCK

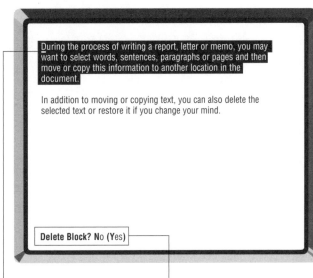

❶ Position the cursor at the first character of the text block you want to delete.

Press **F12** and select the text block with the cursor control keys.

❷ Press **Delete** and the *"Delete Block? No (Yes)"* prompt appears on the screen.

❸ To delete the Block press **Y**.

● The text block is removed from the screen, but is not deleted from your document yet.

❹ To delete the text block permanently, save the document again with the recent changes.

❺ To restore the text block refer to the next page.

DELETE A SENTENCE, PARAGRAPH OR PAGE

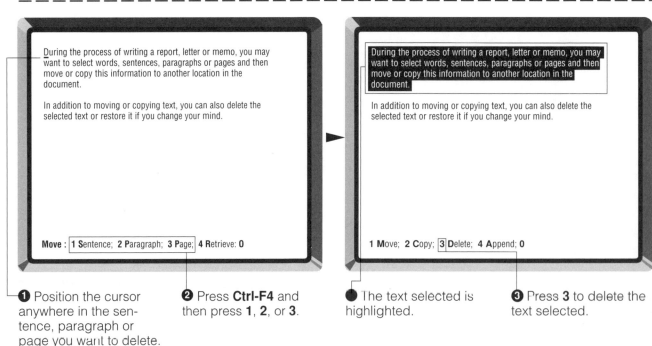

❶ Position the cursor anywhere in the sentence, paragraph or page you want to delete.

❷ Press **Ctrl-F4** and then press **1**, **2**, or **3**.

● The text selected is highlighted.

❸ Press **3** to delete the text selected.

SELECT
TEXT

MOVE
AND COPY
TEXT

**DELETE
AND
RESTORE
TEXT**

HELP

PULL
DOWN
MENUS

CREATE
AND
EDIT A
DOCUMENT

**MOVE, COPY,
DELETE, AND
RESTORE
TEXT**

FORMAT
YOUR
DOCUMENTS

CHECK
YOUR
DOCUMENTS

PRINT
YOUR
DOCUMENTS

MANAGE
YOUR
DOCUMENTS

MERGE
YOUR
DOCUMENTS

RESTORE TEXT

During the process of writing a report, letter or memo, you may want to select words, sentences, paragraphs or pages and then move or copy this information to another location in the document.

In addition to moving or copying text, you can also delete the selected text or restore it if you change your mind.

Undelete: | 1 Restore; | 2 Previous Deletion: 0

During the process of writing a report, letter or memo, you may want to select words, sentences, paragraphs or pages and then move or copy this information to another location in the document._

In addition to moving or copying text, you can also delete the selected text or restore it if you change your mind.

Doc 1 Pg 1 Ln 1.5" Pos 1.9"

● You can recover any or all of the last three text deletions, as long as you have not left WordPerfect.

❶ To display your most recent text deletion, press **F1**.

❷ To restore the deleted text, press **1**.

● The deleted text is restored.

*Note: The text is placed where the cursor was when **F1** was pressed.*

In addition to moving or copying text, you can also delete the selected text or restore it if you change your mind.

Doc 1 Pg 1 Ln 1" Pos 1"

To restore the second text deletion

Press **F1** and then press **2** to display the second text deletion.

Press **1** to restore the displayed text.

To restore the third text deletion

Press **F1** and then press **2** twice to display the third text deletion.

Press **1** to restore the displayed text.

Restored text will be placed wherever the cursor is positioned at the time of the restore.

● The text is removed from the screen, but is not deleted from your document yet.

❹ To delete the text permanently, save the document again with the recent changes.

SETTING MARGINS

SETTING LEFT/RIGHT MARGINS

The left and right margins can be individually set for each or all paragraphs in the document.

If the document is saved, these margins are also saved with the document.

Note: If a new document is opened, the default margin settings of 1" apply.

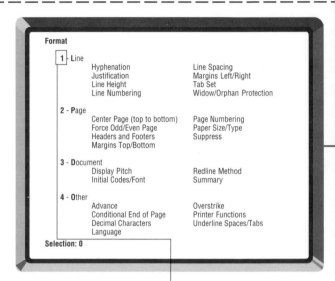

❶ Within your current document move the cursor to the beginning of the line where you want the new margins to start.

❷ Press **Shift-F8** to display the menu above.

❸ Press **1** to display the next screen.

SETTING TOP/BOTTOM MARGINS

The top and bottom margins can be individually set for each or all pages in the document.

If the document is saved, these margins are also saved with the document.

Note: If a new document is opened, the default margin settings of 1" apply.

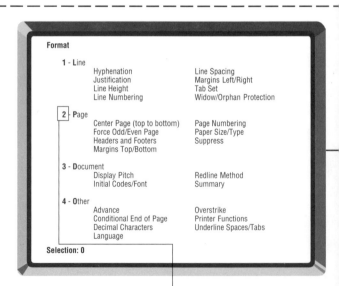

❶ Within your current document move the cursor to top of the page where you want the new margins to start.

❷ Press **Shift-F8** to display the menu above.

❸ Press **2** to display the next screen.

HELP

PULL DOWN MENUS

CREATE AND EDIT A DOCUMENT

MOVE, COPY, DELETE, AND RESTORE TEXT

FORMAT YOUR DOCUMENTS

CHECK YOUR DOCUMENTS

PRINT YOUR DOCUMENTS

MANAGE YOUR DOCUMENTS

MERGE YOUR DOCUMENTS

Format: Line

1 - Hyphenation	No
2 - Hyphenation Zone - Left	10%
Right	4%
3 - Justification	Full
4 - Line Height	Auto
5 - Line Numbering	No
6 - Line Spacing	1
7 - Margins - Left	1"
Right	1"
8 - Tab Set	Rel: -1", every 0.5"
9 - Widow/Orphan Protection	No

Selection: 0

Format: Line

1 - Hyphenation	No
2 - Hyphenation Zone - Left	10%
Right	4%
3 - Justification	Full
4 - Line Height	Auto
5 - Line Numbering	No
6 - Line Spacing	1
7 - Margins - Left	2"
Right	2"
8 - Tab Set	Rel: -1", every 0.5"
9 - Widow/Orphan Protection	No

Selection: 0

4 Press **7** and the cursor moves under the Left Margin 1".

5 Type the size of the new Left Margin and then press **Enter**.

6 Type the size of the new Right Margin and then press **Enter**.

7 To return to your current document, press **F7**.

Format: Page

1 - Center Page (top to bottom)	No
2 - Force Odd/Even Page	
3 - Headers	
4 - Footers	
5 - Margins - Top	1"
Bottom	1"
6 - Page Numbering	
7 - Paper Size	8.5"x11"
Type	Standard
8 - Suppress (this page only)	

Selection: 0

Format: Page

1 - Center Page (top to bottom)	No
2 - Force Odd/Even Page	
3 - Headers	
4 - Footers	
5 - Margins - Top	3"
Bottom	3"
6 - Page Numbering	
7 - Paper Size	8.5"x11"
Type	Standard
8 - Suppress (this page only)	

Selection: 0

4 Press **5** and the cursor moves under the Top Margin 1".

5 Type the size of the new Top Margin and then press **Enter**.

6 Type the size of the new Bottom Margin and then press **Enter**.

7 To return to your current document, press **F7**.

SETTING TABS

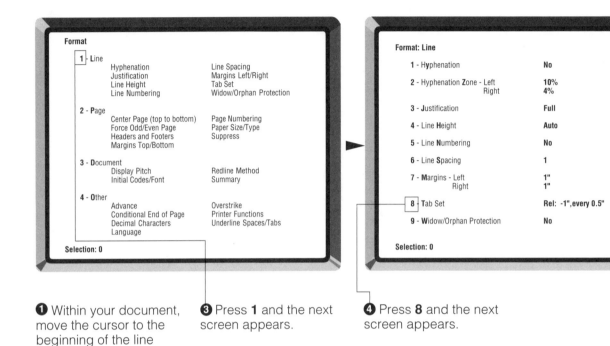

Format

1 - Line

Hyphenation	Line Spacing
Justification	Margins Left/Right
Line Height	Tab Set
Line Numbering	Widow/Orphan Protection

2 - Page

Center Page (top to bottom)	Page Numbering
Force Odd/Even Page	Paper Size/Type
Headers and Footers	Suppress
Margins Top/Bottom	

3 - Document

Display Pitch	Redline Method
Initial Codes/Font	Summary

4 - Other

Advance	Overstrike
Conditional End of Page	Printer Functions
Decimal Characters	Underline Spaces/Tabs
Language	

Selection: 0

Format: Line

1 - Hyphenation	No
2 - Hyphenation Zone - Left	10%
Right	4%
3 - Justification	Full
4 - Line Height	Auto
5 - Line Numbering	No
6 - Line Spacing	1
7 - Margins - Left	1"
Right	1"
8 - Tab Set	Rel: -1",every 0.5"
9 - Widow/Orphan Protection	No

Selection: 0

❶ Within your document, move the cursor to the beginning of the line where you want the new tabs to start.

❷ Press **Shift-F8** to display the menu above.

❸ Press **1** and the next screen appears.

❹ Press **8** and the next screen appears.

The following examples have their tab type set at Absolute.

To save your tab settings and return to the typing area

Press **F7** twice.

DELETE TABS

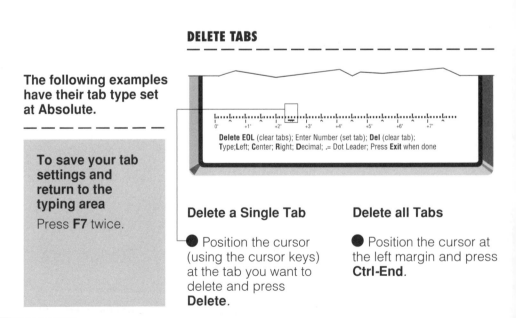

Delete EOL (clear tabs); Enter Number (set tab); **Del** (clear tab);
Type;Left; Center; Right; Decimal; .= Dot Leader; Press **Exit** when done

Delete a Single Tab

● Position the cursor (using the cursor keys) at the tab you want to delete and press **Delete**.

Delete all Tabs

● Position the cursor at the left margin and press **Ctrl-End**.

SETTING
MARGINS

**SETTING
TABS**

INDENT
TEXT

MODIFY
TEXT

CONTROL
TEXT

HELP

PULL
DOWN
MENUS

CREATE
AND
EDIT A
DOCUMENT

MOVE, COPY,
DELETE, AND
RESTORE
TEXT

**FORMAT
YOUR
DOCUMENTS**

CHECK
YOUR
DOCUMENTS

PRINT
YOUR
DOCUMENTS

MANAGE
YOUR
DOCUMENTS

MERGE
YOUR
DOCUMENTS

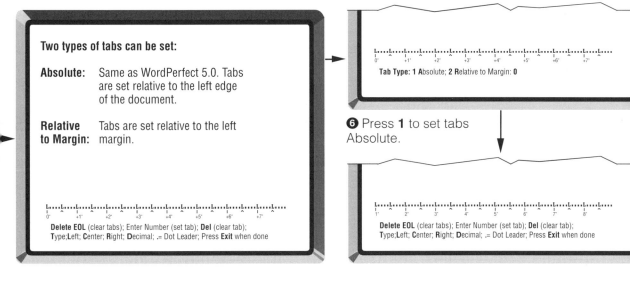

Two types of tabs can be set:

Absolute: Same as WordPerfect 5.0. Tabs are set relative to the left edge of the document.

Relative to Margin: Tabs are set relative to the left margin.

Tab Type: 1 Absolute; **2 R**elative to Margin: **0**

Delete EOL (clear tabs); Enter Number (set tab); **Del** (clear tab);
Type;**L**eft; **C**enter; **R**ight; **D**ecimal; .= Dot Leader; Press **Exit** when done

❻ Press **1** to set tabs Absolute.

Delete EOL (clear tabs); Enter Number (set tab); **Del** (clear tab);
Type;**L**eft; **C**enter; **R**ight; **D**ecimal; .= Dot Leader; Press **Exit** when done

❺ To set Absolute, press **T**.

Note: The standard default setting is Relative to Margin.

● The tab ruler is now set at Absolute.

ADD SINGLE TABS

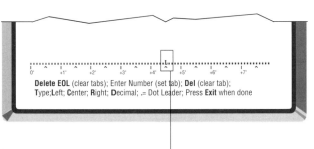

Delete EOL (clear tabs); Enter Number (set tab); **Del** (clear tab);
Type;**L**eft; **C**enter; **R**ight; **D**ecimal; .= Dot Leader; Press **Exit** when done

● Position the cursor where you want to set a new tab. To add:

Left Tab - Press **L**
Right Tab - Press **R**
Decimal Tab - Press **D**
Dot Leader - Press **.**
(period) and then type **L**, **R** or **D**.

● You can also type the position of the tab. If a left tab is required at 4.5 inches, type **4.5** and press **Enter**.

ADD MULTIPLE LEFT TABS

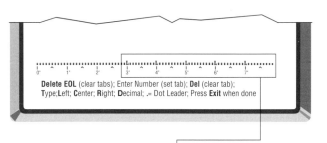

Delete EOL (clear tabs); Enter Number (set tab); **Del** (clear tab);
Type;**L**eft; **C**enter; **R**ight; **D**ecimal; .= Dot Leader; Press **Exit** when done

● Type the distance from the left margin to the first tab in inches, a comma, then the interval in inches between tabs. Press **Enter**.

● For example, to position tabs 1" apart, and starting 3" from the left margin – type **3,1** and press **Enter**.

31

INDENT TEXT

INDENT THE FIRST LINE OF A PARAGRAPH

New Roles for Writer and Designer

➡ The traditional roles of the writer and designer cause many of the problems of the standard book. Traditionally a writer researches the text, writes a draft and gathers up supporting graphics. Then he gives all this material to the designer. The designer arranges these elements into attractive looking pages.

The finished book may look fine, but it is mostly continuous text with pictures inserted wherever the designer placed them.

Doc 1 Pg 1 Ln 1.33" Pos 2"

❶ Position the cursor at the left margin of the line you want to indent. Press **Tab** and the cursor jumps to the first tab setting. In this example, the first tab was set at 2". Start typing.

*Note: To indent further, press **Tab** as many times as required.*

● The indent only applies to the line the cursor is on. The remaining lines of the paragraph are flush to the left margin.

Note:To set tabs refer to page 30.

INDENT THE ENTIRE PARAGRAPH FROM THE LEFT MARGIN

New Roles for Writer and Designer

The traditional roles of the writer and designer cause many of the problems of the standard book. Traditionally a writer researches the text, writes a draft and gathers up supporting graphics. Then he gives all this material to the designer. The designer arranges these elements into attractive looking pages.

The finished book may look fine, but it is mostly continuous text with pictures inserted wherever the designer placed them.

Doc 1 Pg 1 Ln 1.33" Pos 2"

❶ Position the cursor at the left margin of the first line of the paragraph you want to indent. Press **F4** and the cursor jumps to the first tab. In this example, the first tab was set at 2". Start typing.

● The indent applies to all lines in the paragraph including and below the cursor.

❷ Press **Enter** to turn off the indent. The cursor also moves to the left margin of the next line.

To remove indent settings

Place the cursor on the first character of text in the first indented line.

Press **Backspace** to return to your original cursor position.

SETTING
MARGINS

SETTING
TABS

**INDENT
TEXT**

MODIFY
TEXT

CONTROL
TEXT

HELP

PULL
DOWN
MENUS

CREATE
AND
EDIT A
DOCUMENT

MOVE, COPY,
DELETE, AND
RESTORE
TEXT

**FORMAT
YOUR
DOCUMENTS**

CHECK
YOUR
DOCUMENTS

PRINT
YOUR
DOCUMENTS

MANAGE
YOUR
DOCUMENTS

MERGE
YOUR
DOCUMENTS

INDENT THE ENTIRE
PARAGRAPH FROM BOTH MARGINS

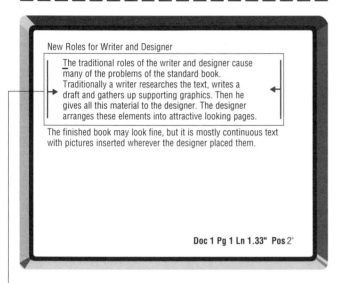

New Roles for Writer and Designer

The traditional roles of the writer and designer cause many of the problems of the standard book. Traditionally a writer researches the text, writes a draft and gathers up supporting graphics. Then he gives all this material to the designer. The designer arranges these elements into attractive looking pages.

The finished book may look fine, but it is mostly continuous text with pictures inserted wherever the designer placed them.

Doc 1 Pg 1 Ln 1.33" Pos 2"

❶ Position the cursor at the left margin of the first line of the paragraph you want to indent from both margins. Press **Shift-F4**. Start typing.

Note: If the first **Absolute** *tab is set at 2", the left indent from the right side of the page is automatically set at 2".*

If the first **Relative** *tab is set at 2", the left indent from the right margin is automatically set at 2".*

● The indent applies to all lines in the paragraph including and below the cursor.

❷ Press **Enter** to turn off the indent from both margins. The cursor also moves to the left margin of the next line.

Indent existing paragraphs from the left or both margins

● **Indent first line**

Position the cursor on the first character of the line and press **Tab**. If the line is part of a paragraph, press ↓ to reformat the paragraph.

● **Indent entire paragraph from left margin**

Position the cursor on the first character of the paragraph and press **F4**. Then press ↓ to reformat the paragraph.

● **Indent entire paragraph from both margins**

Position the cursor on the first character of the first line of the paragraph and press **Shift-F4**. Then press ↓ to reformat the paragraph.

MODIFY TEXT

BOLDFACE TEXT

New Roles for Writer and Designer

The traditional roles of the writer and designer cause many of the problems of the standard book. Traditionally a writer researches the text, writes a draft and gathers up supporting graphics. Then he gives all this material to the designer. The designer arranges these elements into attractive looking pages.

The finished book may look fine, but it is mostly continuous text with pictures inserted wherever the designer placed them.

Doc 1 Pg 1 Ln 1" Pos 1"

UNDERLINE TEXT

New Roles for Writer and Designer

The traditional roles of the writer and designer cause many of the problems of the standard book. Traditionally a writer researches the text, writes a draft and gathers up supporting graphics. Then he gives all this material to the designer. The designer arranges these elements into attractive looking pages.

The finished book may look fine, but it is mostly continuous text with pictures inserted wherever the designer placed them.

Doc 1 Pg 1 Ln 1" Pos 1"

For new text

❶ To boldface text, position the cursor where you want the type to start. Then press **F6** and begin typing.

❷ To turn off boldface, press **F6** again.

For existing text

❶ To boldface the second paragraph, position the cursor at the beginning of the first word in the text block. Press **F12** and highlight the paragraph with the cursor keys, then press **F6** to boldface the paragraph.

For new text

❶ To underline text, position the cursor where you want the underline type to start, then press **F8** and begin typing.

❷ To turn off Underline, press **F8** again.

For existing text

❶ To underline existing text, position the cursor at the beginning of the first word in the text block. Press **F12** and highlight the paragraph with the cursor keys, then press **F8** to underline the paragraph.

SETTING
MARGINS

SETTING
TABS

INDENT
TEXT

**MODIFY
TEXT**

CONTROL
TEXT

HELP

PULL
DOWN
MENUS

CREATE
AND
EDIT A
DOCUMENT

MOVE, COPY,
DELETE, AND
RESTORE
TEXT

**FORMAT
YOUR
DOCUMENTS**

CHECK
YOUR
DOCUMENTS

PRINT
YOUR
DOCUMENTS

MANAGE
YOUR
DOCUMENTS

MERGE
YOUR
DOCUMENTS

CHANGE BASE FONT

New Roles for Writer and Designer

The traditional roles of the writer and designer cause many of the problems of the standard book. Traditionally a writer researches the text, writes a draft and gathers up supporting graphics. Then he gives all this material to the designer. The designer arranges these elements into attractive looking pages.

The finished book may look fine, but it is mostly continuous text with pictures inserted wherever the designer placed them.

1 **S**ize; 2 **A**ppearance; 3 **N**ormal; 4 **B**ase Font; 5 Print **C**olour: 0

Base Font

Boldface PS
Boldface PS Dbl Wide
Boldface PS Dbl Wide Super/Sub
Boldface PS Super/Sub
Courier 10 Dbl Wide
Courier 10 Dbl Wide Super/Sub
Courier 10 Dbl Super/Sub
Courier 12
Courier 12 Dbl Wide
Courier 12 Dbl Wide Super/Sub
Courier 12 Dbl Super/Sub
* Courier 17
Courier 17 Dbl Wide
Courier 17 Dbl Wide Super/Sub
Courier 17 Dbl Super/Sub

1 **S**elect; **N** **N**ame search: 1

❶ Using the cursor keys, position the cursor where you want the new base font to begin.

❷ Press **Ctrl-F8** and the prompt above appears.

❸ Press **4** and a list of available fonts for your printer are displayed on the next screen.

❹ Choose the base font required with the cursor control keys (in this example Courier 17 was selected).

❺ Press **Enter** to select the new base font and return to your document.

TO VIEW THE NEW BASE FONT

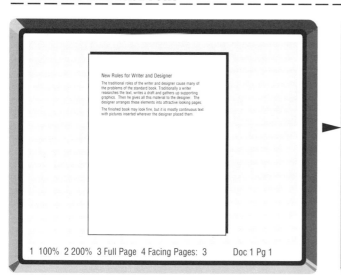

1 100% 2 200% 3 Full Page 4 Facing Pages: 3   Doc 1 Pg 1

New Roles for V

The traditional roles
the problems of the
researches the text,
graphics. Then he

1 100% 2 200% 3 Full Page 4 Facing Pages: 3   Doc 1 Pg 1

❶ Press **Shift-F7** and then **6** to view the page.

❷ Press **2** to view document at 200%.

❸ Press **F7** to leave the view.

ADJUST TEXT FLUSH RIGHT

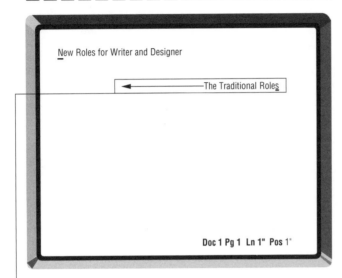

New Roles for Writer and Designer

The Traditional Roles

Doc 1 Pg 1 Ln 1" Pos 1"

For new text

❶ Press **Alt-F6** and the cursor jumps to the right margin. Start typing and note that the cursor remains stationary as the new type created flows to the left.

For existing text

❶ Move the cursor to the left margin of the line of text you want to flush right. Press **Alt-F6** to move the text flush right.

Press ⬇ to automatically realign text.

To switch off flush right
Press **Enter.**

CENTER A LINE

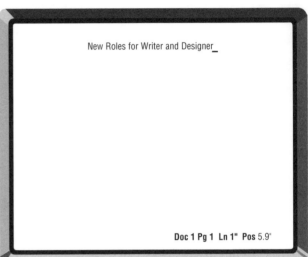

New Roles for Writer and Designer

Doc 1 Pg 1 Ln 1" Pos 5.9"

For new text

❶ Position the cursor at the left margin and then press **Shift-F6**. Start typing and the line is centered as characters are added.

For existing text

❶ Move the cursor to the first character of the line you want to center. Press **Shift-F6** to center the line.

Press ⬇ to automatically realign text.

To switch off center a line
Press **Enter.**

SETTING
MARGINS

SETTING
TABS

INDENT
TEXT

MODIFY
TEXT

**CONTROL
TEXT**

HELP

PULL
DOWN
MENUS

CREATE
AND
EDIT A
DOCUMENT

MOVE, COPY,
DELETE, AND
RESTORE
TEXT

**FORMAT
YOUR
DOCUMENTS**

CHECK
YOUR
DOCUMENTS

PRINT
YOUR
DOCUMENTS

MANAGE
YOUR
DOCUMENTS

MERGE
YOUR
DOCUMENTS

LINE SPACING

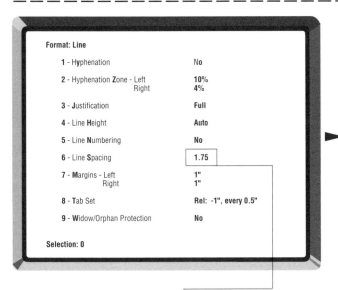

Format: Line

1 - Hyphenation	No
2 - Hyphenation Zone - Left	10%
Right	4%
3 - Justification	Full
4 - Line Height	Auto
5 - Line Numbering	No
6 - Line Spacing	1.75
7 - Margins - Left	1"
Right	1"
8 - Tab Set	Rel: -1", every 0.5"
9 - Widow/Orphan Protection	No

Selection: 0

New Roles for Writer and Designer

The traditional roles of the writer and designer cause many of
the problems of the standard book. Traditionally a writer
researches the text, writes a draft and gathers up supporting
graphics. Then he gives all this material to the designer. The
designer arranges these elements into attractive looking pages.

The finished book may look fine, but it is mostly continous text
with pictures inserted wherever the designer placed them.

Doc 1 Pg 1 Ln 1" Pos 1"

❶ Place the cursor at
the left margin of the first
line where the spacing is
to change.

❷ Press **Shift-F8** and
then **1** to display the
menu above.

❸ Press **6** and the cursor
moves under the *"1"*.
Type in the new line
spacing (for example
1.75). Then press **Enter**.

*Note: The line spacing
can be specified with an
accuracy of two decimal
places.*

❹ To return to your
current document,
press **F7**.

SEARCH

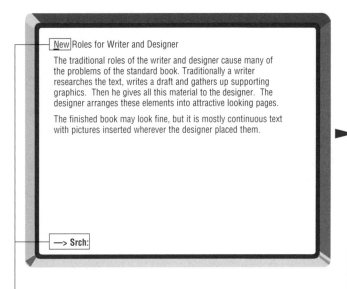

New Roles for Writer and Designer

The traditional roles of the writer and designer cause many of the problems of the standard book. Traditionally a writer researches the text, writes a draft and gathers up supporting graphics. Then he gives all this material to the designer. The designer arranges these elements into attractive looking pages.

The finished book may look fine, but it is mostly continuous text with pictures inserted wherever the designer placed them.

—> Srch:

New Roles for Writer and Designer

The traditional roles of the writer and designer cause many of the problems of the standard book. Traditionally a writer researches the text, writes a draft and gathers up supporting graphics. Then he gives all this material to the designer. The designer arranges these elements into attractive looking pages.

The finished book may look fine, but it is mostly continuous text with pictures inserted wherever the designer placed them.

—> Srch: designer

Forward Search

● Start the search from the cursor to the document end by pressing **F2**. The prompt " → Srch:" appears.

Backward Search

● Start the search from the cursor to the document beginning by pressing **Shift-F2**. The prompt "← Srch:" appears.

❶ Type in the character, word or sentence (called a string) that you want to identify in the document (for example *"designer"*).

Note: The maximum size of your search string can not exceed 60 characters.

SEARCH GUIDELINES

● If you search for "designer" in lowercase you may find designer, Designer or DESIGNER.

● If you search for "DESIGNER" in uppercase you will only find DESIGNER.

● If you search for "place" you may find replace, commonplace, placement, places, etc.

HELP

PULL
DOWN
MENUS

CREATE
AND
EDIT A
DOCUMENT

MOVE, COPY,
DELETE, AND
RESTORE
TEXT

FORMAT
YOUR
DOCUMENTS

CHECK
YOUR
DOCUMENTS

PRINT
YOUR
DOCUMENTS

MANAGE
YOUR
DOCUMENTS

MERGE
YOUR
DOCUMENTS

New Roles for Writer and Designer

The traditional roles of the writer and designer cause many of
the problems of the standard book. Traditionally a writer
researches the text, writes a draft and gathers up supporting
graphics. Then he gives all this material to the designer. The
designer arranges these elements into attractive looking pages.

The finished book may look fine, but it is mostly continuous text
with pictures inserted wherever the designer placed them.

Doc 1 Pg 1 Ln 1" Pos 5.4"

❷ To initiate the search press **F2.**

● WordPerfect searches for *"designer"* and stops the first time it appears.

❸ To search for each successive appearance of *"designer"*, press **F2** twice.

To search for a previous appearance, press **Shift-F2** twice.

To cancel search
Press **F1**.

Resetting the cursor
Press **Ctrl-Home** twice to reset cursor to its position prior to starting the search.

● To make sure the word you are searching for is not part of a larger word, enter a space at both ends of the word. For example to search for "place" enter "<space>place<space>".

REPLACE

New Roles for Writer and Designer

The traditional roles of the writer and designer cause many of
the problems of the standard book. Traditionally a writer
researches the text, writes a draft and gathers up supporting
graphics. Then he gives all this material to the designer. The
designer arranges these elements into attractive looking pages.

The finished book may look fine, but it is mostly continuous text
with pictures inserted wherever the designer placed them.

w/Confirm? No (Yes)

New Roles for Writer and Designer

The traditional roles of the writer and designer cause many of
the problems of the standard book. Traditionally a writer
researches the text, writes a draft and gathers up supporting
graphics. Then he gives all this material to the designer. The
designer arranges these elements into attractive looking pages.

The finished book may look fine, but it is mostly continuous text
with pictures inserted wherever the designer placed them.

—> **Srch:** designer

❶ Position the cursor at
the left margin of the line
where you want the
replace function to begin.
Then press **Alt-F2**.

❷ The prompt
"w/Confirm? No (Yes)"
appears on the screen.

Press **N** - All selected
words are replaced at the
same time.

Press **Y** - The cursor
stops at each word to be
replaced. You can then
decide which of the
selected words require
replacement.

❸ For this example,
press **Y**.

❹ The prompt *"→Srch:"*
appears on the screen.
Type in the word you
want replaced (for
example *"designer"*).
Then press **Alt-F2.**

The Replace func-
tion is normally
used for words,
however, any text
string (character,
sentence, para-
graph) or codes
can apply.

HELP

PULL
DOWN
MENUS

CREATE
AND
EDIT A
DOCUMENT

MOVE, COPY,
DELETE, AND
RESTORE
TEXT

FORMAT
YOUR
DOCUMENTS

**CHECK
YOUR
DOCUMENTS**

PRINT
YOUR
DOCUMENTS

MANAGE
YOUR
DOCUMENTS

MERGE
YOUR
DOCUMENTS

New Roles for Writer and Designer

The traditional roles of the writer and designer cause many of
the problems of the standard book. Traditionally a writer
researches the text, writes a draft and gathers up supporting
graphics. Then he gives all this material to the designer. The
designer arranges these elements into attractive looking pages.

The finished book may look fine, but it is mostly continuous text
with pictures inserted wherever the designer placed them.

Replace with: artist

New Roles for Writer and Designer

The traditional roles of the writer and designer cause many of
the problems of the standard book. Traditionally a writer
researches the text, writes a draft and gathers up supporting
graphics. Then he gives all this material to the designer. The
designer arranges these elements into attractive looking pages.

The finished book may look fine, but it is mostly continuous text
with pictures inserted wherever the designer placed them.

w/Confirm? No (Yes)

❺ The prompt *"Replace
with:"* appears on the
screen. Type in the word
to replace the searched
term (for example *"artist"*).
Then press **Alt-F2**.

❻ The cursor will be
positioned at the first
word it found during the
search.

❼ The prompt *"Confirm?
No (Yes)"* appears
because **Y** was selected
in step **❷**. Press **Y** to
change the word, or **N**
for it to stay the same.
WordPerfect then
searches for the next
occurrence of *"designer"*
in the document.

*Note: If you pressed **N**
when the prompt "w/
Confirm? **N**o (**Y**es)"
appeared in step **❷**,
the word "artist" replaces
"designer" throughout
the entire document.*

To cancel replace
Press **F1**.

41

SPELLCHECK

New Roles for Writer and Designer

The traditional roles of the writer and designer cause many fo the problems of the standard book.

The finished book may look fine, but it is mostly continuous text with pictures inserted wherever the designer placed them. The Hypergraphics process solves this problem.

Check: 1 Word; **2** Page; **3** Document; **4** New Sup. Dictionary; **5** Look Up; **6** Count: **0**

New Roles for Writer and Designer

The traditional roles of the writer and designer cause many **fo** the problems of the standard book.

The finished book may look fine, but it is mostly continuous text with pictures inserted wherever the designer placed them. The Hypergraphics process solves this problem.

Doc 1 Pg 1 Ln 1.33" Pos 7"

A. f	B. fc	C. fd
D. fe	E. fl	F. fm
G. fob	H. foe	I. fog
J. fol	K. fop	L. for
M. fox	N. fr	O. fro
P. fs	Q. ft	R. fu
S. of	T. o	U. fay
V. fee	W. feu	X. few

Press **Enter** for more words

Not Found: 1 Skip Once; **2** Skip; **3** Add; **4** Edit; **5** Look Up; **6** Ignore Numbers: **0**

To spellcheck a word

Place the cursor under the word you want to spellcheck. Press **Ctrl-F2** and then **1**. If the word is correctly spelled, the cursor jumps to the beginning of the next word.

If the word is incorrectly spelled, a list of alternative spellings appears (refer to next screen). To replace the word, press the letter in front of correctly spelled word.

To spellcheck a page

Place the cursor anywhere on the page you want to spellcheck. Press **Ctrl-F2** and then **2**. Refer to ❶.

To spellcheck a document

Press **Ctrl-F2** and then **3**. Refer to ❶.

To check the number of words in the document

Press **Ctrl-F2** and then **6**.

❶ WordPerfect begins to spellcheck the page or document and identifies the characters *"fo"* as being incorrectly spelled.

The program offers a list of possible correct spellings of *"fo"*.

❷ If you would like to replace *"fo"* with *"of"*, type **S** and WordPerfect corrects the word and continues checking the page.

or

If the characters *"fo"* are correct, press **2** and WordPerfect continues checking the page.

To cancel spellcheck
Press **F1**.

HELP

PULL
DOWN
MENUS

CREATE
AND
EDIT A
DOCUMENT

MOVE, COPY,
DELETE, AND
RESTORE
TEXT

FORMAT
YOUR
DOCUMENTS

CHECK
YOUR
DOCUMENTS

PRINT
YOUR
DOCUMENTS

MANAGE
YOUR
DOCUMENTS

MERGE
YOUR
DOCUMENTS

New Roles for Writer and Designer

The traditional roles of the writer and designer cause many of the problems of the standard book.

The finished book may look fine, but it is mostly continuous text with pictures inserted wherever the designer placed them. The Hypergraphics process solves this problem.

Doc 1 Pg 1 Ln 2.17" Pos 1"

Not Found: 1 Skip Once; 2 Skip; 3 Add; 4 Edit; 5 Look Up; 6 Ignore Numbers: 0

New Roles for Writer and Designer

The traditional roles of the writer and designer cause many of the problems of the standard book.

The finished book may look fine, but it is mostly continuous text with pictures inserted wherever the designer placed them. The Hypergraphics process solves this problem.

Word count: 49   Press any key to continue

❸ WordPerfect identifies the word *"Hypergraphics"* as not being in its dictionary.

❹ To add the word *"Hypergraphics"* to WordPerfect's Supplementary Dictionary, press **3**.

WordPerfect adds Hypergraphics to its dictionary and continues to spellcheck the document.

❺ To make these changes permanent, press **F7** to save the document.

SPELLCHECK OPTIONS

Skip One	- Ignores this occurrence of the word. The next time the word appears in this document it is highlighted.	**Edit**	- Allows the user to manually change the word.
Skip	- Ignores all occurrences of the word in this document during the spellcheck.	**Lookup**	- To find other alternative spellings, look up part of this word..
Add	- Adds the word to the Supplemental Dictionary so it is recognized in future.	**Ignore Number**	- Ignore number/letter combinations.

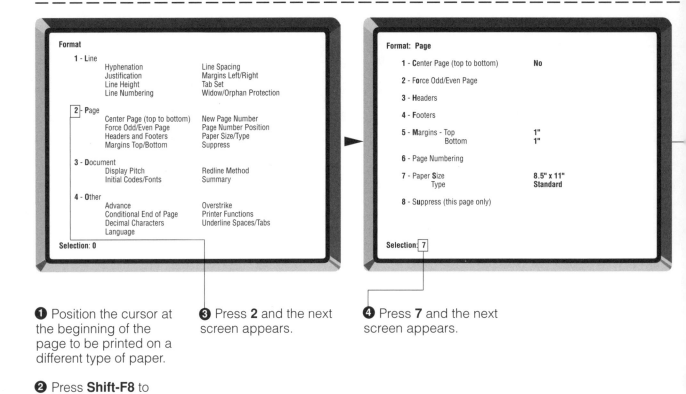

Format

1 - Line
- Hyphenation
- Justification
- Line Height
- Line Numbering
- Line Spacing
- Margins Left/Right
- Tab Set
- Widow/Orphan Protection

2 - Page
- Center Page (top to bottom)
- Force Odd/Even Page
- Headers and Footers
- Margins Top/Bottom
- New Page Number
- Page Number Position
- Paper Size/Type
- Suppress

3 - Document
- Display Pitch
- Initial Codes/Fonts
- Redline Method
- Summary

4 - Other
- Advance
- Conditional End of Page
- Decimal Characters
- Language
- Overstrike
- Printer Functions
- Underline Spaces/Tabs

Selection: 0

Format: Page

1 - Center Page (top to bottom)	No
2 - Force Odd/Even Page	
3 - Headers	
4 - Footers	
5 - Margins - Top	1"
Bottom	1"
6 - Page Numbering	
7 - Paper Size	8.5" x 11"
Type	Standard
8 - Suppress (this page only)	

Selection: 7

❶ Position the cursor at the beginning of the page to be printed on a different type of paper.

❷ Press **Shift-F8** to display the screen above.

❸ Press **2** and the next screen appears.

❹ Press **7** and the next screen appears.

SELECT
PAPER AND
FORM SIZES

VIEW
DOCUMENT

PRINT
DISPLAYED
DOCUMENT

HELP

PULL
DOWN
MENUS

CREATE
AND
EDIT A
DOCUMENT

MOVE, COPY,
DELETE, AND
RESTORE
TEXT

FORMAT
YOUR
DOCUMENTS

CHECK
YOUR
DOCUMENTS

PRINT
YOUR
DOCUMENTS

MANAGE
YOUR
DOCUMENTS

MERGE
YOUR
DOCUMENTS

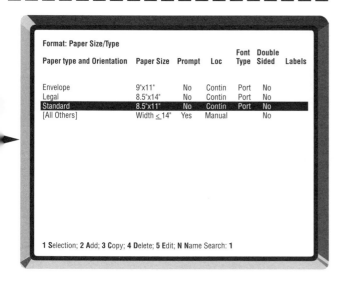

Format: Paper Size/Type

Paper type and Orientation	Paper Size	Prompt	Loc	Font Type	Double Sided	Labels
Envelope	9"x11"	No	Contin	Port	No	
Legal	8.5"x14"	No	Contin	Port	No	
Standard	8.5"x11"	No	Contin	Port	No	
[All Others]	Width ≤ 14"	Yes	Manual		No	

1 Selection; 2 Add; 3 Copy; 4 Delete; 5 Edit; N Name Search: 1

❺ Use the cursor control keys ⬇ and ⬆ to highlight the paper size or form you require.

❻ Press **Enter**.

❼ Press **F7** to return to the typing screen.

SOME PRINT FORMS ARE PRE-DEFINED

If you need to use a form that does not appear on the screen above, Press **2** to *"Add"* a form and refer to your WordPerfect 5.1 documentation.

VIEW DOCUMENT

Press **Shift-F7** and then **6** to view the entire page. Viewing the document before printing can save paper and your valuable time.

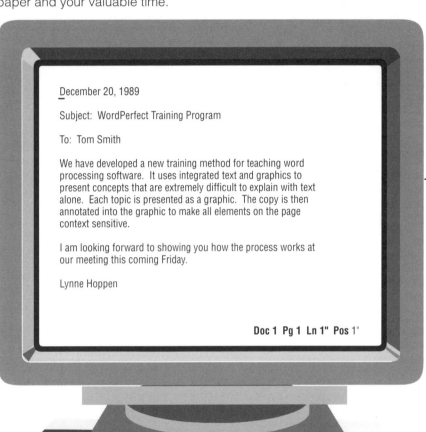

December 20, 1989

Subject: WordPerfect Training Program

To: Tom Smith

We have developed a new training method for teaching word processing software. It uses integrated text and graphics to present concepts that are extremely difficult to explain with text alone. Each topic is presented as a graphic. The copy is then annotated into the graphic to make all elements on the page context sensitive.

I am looking forward to showing you how the process works at our meeting this coming Friday.

Lynne Hoppen

Doc 1 Pg 1 Ln 1" Pos 1"

SELECT
PAPER AND
FORM SIZES

**VIEW
DOCUMENT**

PRINT
DISPLAYED
DOCUMENT

HELP

PULL
DOWN
MENUS

CREATE
AND
EDIT A
DOCUMENT

MOVE, COPY,
DELETE, AND
RESTORE
TEXT

FORMAT
YOUR
DOCUMENTS

CHECK
YOUR
DOCUMENTS

**PRINT
YOUR
DOCUMENTS**

MANAGE
YOUR
DOCUMENTS

MERGE
YOUR
DOCUMENTS

When in any of the 3 other viewing modes, press **3** to return to viewing the entire page.

Press **1** to view document at 100%. To scan through the page, press the ⬇ or ⬆ cursor control keys.

1 100% 2 200% 3 Full Page 4 Facing Pages: 3   Doc 1 Pg 1

1 100% 2 200% 3 Full Page 4 Facing Pages: 1   Doc 1 Pg 1

December 20, 1989

Subject: WordPerfect Training Progra

To: Tom Smith

We have developed a new training me
processing software. It uses integrate
present concepts that are extremely d

1 100% 2 200% 3 Full Page 4 Facing Pages: 2   Doc 1 Pg 1

1 100% 2 200% 3 Full Page 4 Facing Pages: 4   Doc 1 Pg 2-3

Press **2** to view document at 200%. To scan through the page, press the ⬇ or ⬆ cursor control keys.

Press **4** to view both the current and facing pages simultaneously.

To view other pages in the document
Press **PgUp** or **PgDn**.

To return to document from viewing mode
Press **F7**.

PRINT DISPLAYED DOCUMENT

PRINT ANY SINGLE PAGE WITHIN YOUR DOCUMENT

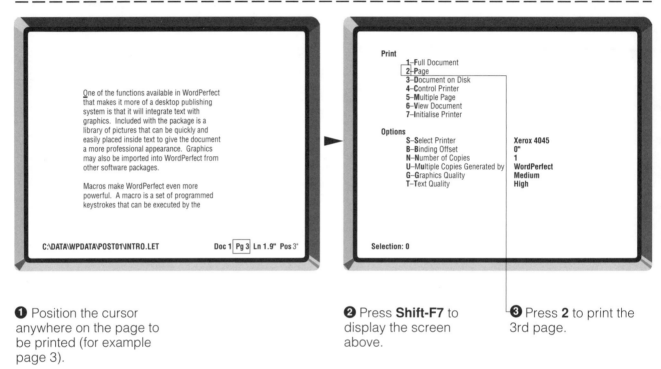

❶ Position the cursor anywhere on the page to be printed (for example page 3).

❷ Press **Shift-F7** to display the screen above.

❸ Press **2** to print the 3rd page.

PRINT YOUR ENTIRE DOCUMENT

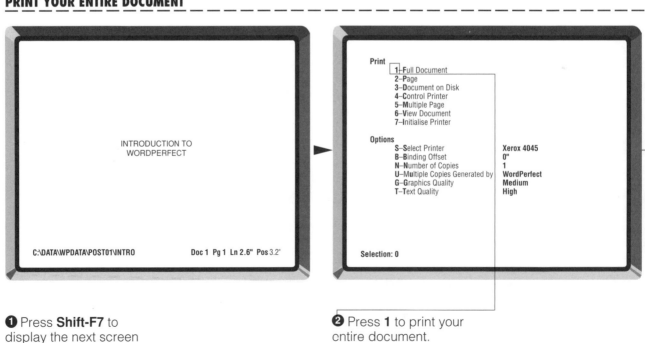

❶ Press **Shift-F7** to display the next screen above.

❷ Press **1** to print your entire document.

SELECT
PAPER AND
FORM SIZES

VIEW
DOCUMENT

**PRINT
DISPLAYED
DOCUMENT**

HELP

PULL
DOWN
MENUS

CREATE
AND
EDIT A
DOCUMENT

MOVE, COPY,
DELETE, AND
RESTORE
TEXT

FORMAT
YOUR
DOCUMENTS

CHECK
YOUR
DOCUMENTS

**PRINT
YOUR
DOCUMENTS**

MANAGE
YOUR
DOCUMENTS

MERGE
YOUR
DOCUMENTS

PRINT MULTIPLE PAGES WITHIN YOUR DOCUMENT

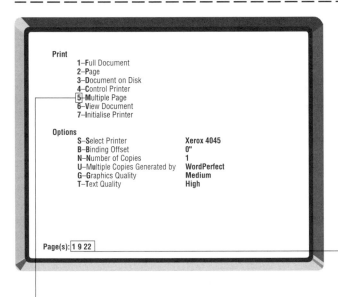

```
Print
     1–Full Document
     2–Page
     3–Document on Disk
     4–Control Printer
     5–Multiple Page
     6–View Document
     7–Initialise Printer

Options
     S–Select Printer              Xerox 4045
     B–Binding Offset              0"
     N–Number of Copies            1
     U–Multiple Copies Generated by  WordPerfect
     G–Graphics Quality            Medium
     T–Text Quality                High




Page(s): 1 9 22
```

❷ **To print random pages**

Type the page numbers, separated by spaces (for example **1 9 22**). Then press **Enter**.

or

❸ **To print a group of sequential pages**

Type the first and last pages of the sequence separated by a dash (for example **6-11**). Then press **Enter**.

❶ Press **5** to select multiple pages and the prompt *"Page(s):"* appears.

Page 1

INTRODUCTION TO
WORDPERFECT

Page 2

WordPerfect is a highly advanced word processing system that allows the user to work with basic desktop publishing functions. It is one of the most popular software packages in the marketplace.

WordPerfect uses Function Keys to access the many capabilities it offers. For example, to access the online Help function, a user simply presses the F3 key. Function keys have multiple capabilities. A template is available to assist the user in remembering the options associated with each key.

WordPerfect also contains a comprehensive dictionary that allows users to Spellcheck their work. The user can even create a "customized" dictionary that will include words and names they work with regularly.

A thesaurus is also included in the package. This is a very useful aid, especially for those doing extensive writing.

Page 3 (Last Page)

One of the functions available in WordPerfect that makes it more of a desktop publishing system is that it will integrate text with graphics. Included with the package is a library of pictures that can be quickly and easily placed inside text to give the document a more professional appearance. Graphics may also be imported into WordPerfect from other software packages.

Macros make WordPerfect even more powerful. A macro is a set of programmed keystrokes that can be executed by the machine more quickly than they could be done by the user.

49

● Press **F5** and then **Enter** to list all your files in the current directory.

● To list files in other directories, press **F5**, type the directory path and file name.

For example: type *"C:\DATA\WPDATA\POST02"* and then press **Enter**.

Note: This does not change the current directory.

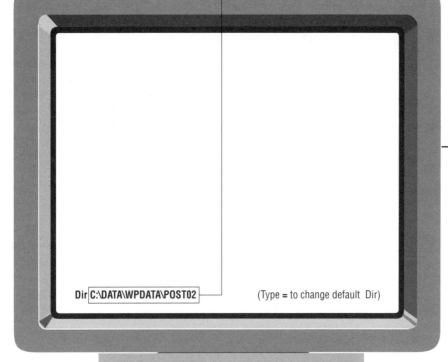

Dir C:\DATA\WPDATA\POST02   (Type = to change default Dir)

INTRODUCTION

DELETE/
MOVE OR
RENAME/
PRINT/LOOK

OTHER
DIRECTORY/
COPY/NAME
SEARCH

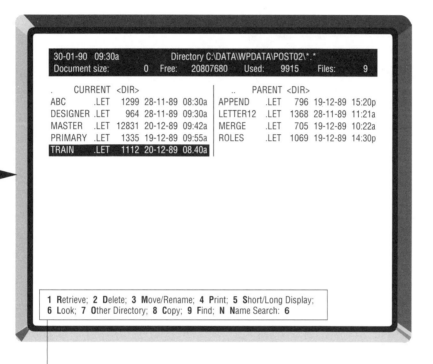

```
30-01-90  09:30a              Directory C:\DATA\WPDATA\POST02\*.*
Document size:      0   Free:   20807680   Used:    9915   Files:      9

.       CURRENT  <DIR>              ..      PARENT  <DIR>
ABC        .LET   1299  28-11-89  08:30a   APPEND    .LET    796  19-12-89  15:20p
DESIGNER   .LET    964  28-11-89  09:30a   LETTER12  .LET   1368  28-11-89  11:21a
MASTER     .LET  12831  20-12-89  09:42a   MERGE     .LET    705  19-12-89  10:22a
PRIMARY    .LET   1335  19-12-89  09:55a   ROLES     .LET   1069  19-12-89  14:30p
TRAIN      .LET   1112  20-12-89  08.40a



1 Retrieve; 2 Delete; 3 Move/Rename; 4 Print; 5 Short/Long Display;
6 Look; 7 Other Directory; 8 Copy; 9 Find; N Name Search: 6
```

List files menu

● This menu allows you to perform many of the DOS file/document management commands within WordPerfect.

To select a command, press the number to the left of the command or the highlighted first letter of the command.

1 **R**etrieve; **2** **D**el
6 **L**ook; **7** **O**ther

To return to your document
Press **F7**.

HELP

PULL
DOWN
MENUS

CREATE
AND
EDIT A
DOCUMENT

MOVE, COPY,
DELETE, AND
RESTORE
TEXT

FORMAT
YOUR
DOCUMENTS

CHECK
YOUR
DOCUMENTS

PRINT
YOUR
DOCUMENTS

MANAGE
YOUR
DOCUMENTS

MERGE
YOUR
DOCUMENTS

DELETE MOVE OR RENAME

PRINT LOOK

DELETE

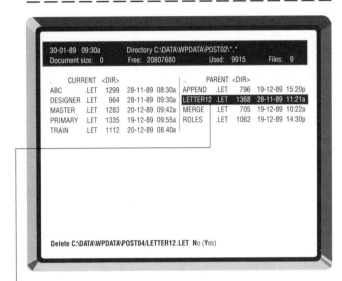

```
30-01-89  09:30a        Directory C:\DATA\WPDATA\POST02\*.*
Document size:  0       Free:  20807680        Used:  9915       Files:  9

.    CURRENT  <DIR>              ..    PARENT  <DIR>
ABC       .LET   1299  28-11-89 08:30a   APPEND    .LET    796  19-12-89 15:20p
DESIGNER  .LET    964  28-11-89 09:30a   LETTER12  .LET   1368  28-11-89 11:21a
MASTER    .LET   1283  20-12-89 09:42a   MERGE     .LET    705  19-12-89 10:22a
PRIMARY   .LET   1335  19-12-89 09:55a   ROLES     .LET   1062  19-12-89 14:30p
TRAIN     .LET   1112  20-12-89 08.40a




Delete C:\DATA\WPDATA\POST04/LETTER12.LET  No (Yes)
```

❶ Use the cursor control keys to highlight the file or directory you want deleted (for example LETTER12.LET).

❷ Press **2** and then **Y** to delete the file or directory.

● *Before a directory can be deleted, all files contained in that directory must be deleted.*

If the message "ERROR: Directory not empty" is displayed, files still remain in the directory.

These files must be deleted before the directory can be deleted.

MOVE OR RENAME

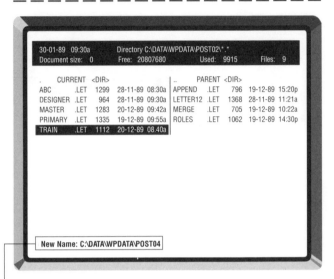

```
30-01-89  09:30a        Directory C:\DATA\WPDATA\POST02\*.*
Document size:  0       Free:  20807680        Used:  9915       Files:  9

.    CURRENT  <DIR>              ..    PARENT  <DIR>
ABC       .LET   1299  28-11-89 08:30a   APPEND    .LET    796  19-12-89 15:20p
DESIGNER  .LET    964  28-11-89 09:30a   LETTER12  .LET   1368  28-11-89 11:21a
MASTER    .LET   1283  20-12-89 09:42a   MERGE     .LET    705  19-12-89 10:22a
PRIMARY   .LET   1335  19-12-89 09:55a   ROLES     .LET   1062  19-12-89 14:30p
TRAIN     .LET   1112  20-12-89 08.40a



New Name: C:\DATA\WPDATA\POST04
```

Move a file

❶ Use the cursor control keys to highlight the file to be moved (for example *"TRAIN .LET"*).

❷ Press **3** to move the file.

❸ Type the directory path the file is being moved to followed by the file name (for example C:\DATA\WPDATA\ POST04\TRAIN.LET) and press **Enter**.

Rename a file

❶ Use the cursor control keys to highlight the file to be renamed.

❷ Press **3** to rename the file.

❸ Type the new file name and press **Enter**.

Retrieve

The Retrieve command is described on page 12.

To cancel delete/ move/rename/print/ look

Press **F1**.

HELP

PULL DOWN MENUS

CREATE AND EDIT A DOCUMENT

MOVE, COPY, DELETE, AND RESTORE TEXT

FORMAT YOUR DOCUMENTS

CHECK YOUR DOCUMENTS

PRINT YOUR DOCUMENTS

MANAGE YOUR DOCUMENTS

MERGE YOUR DOCUMENTS

PRINT

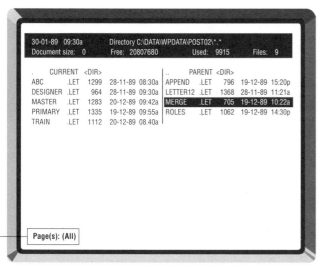

❶ Use the cursor control keys to highlight the file to be printed (for example *"MERGE.LET"*).

❷ Press **4** and the prompt *"Page(s): (All)"* appears.

To print all pages
Press **Enter**.

To print a single page
Type the page number (for example **3**) and press **Enter**.

To print random pages
Type the page numbers, separated by spaces (for example **1 9 22**) and press **Enter**.

To print a group of sequential pages
Type the first and last pages of the sequence separated by a dash (for example **6-11**) and press **Enter**.

LOOK

❶ Use the cursor control keys to highlight the file to be displayed (for example *"PRIMARY.LET"*).

❷ Press **6** to look at the file. Access to the file is quick, but it cannot be edited.

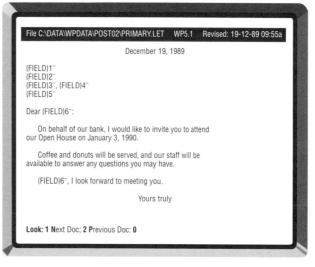

● The cursor control keys work normally.

● Press **S** to scroll through the document. To stop scrolling press **S** again.

❸ Press **F7** to return to the List Files menu.

OTHER DIRECTORY

```
30-01-90  09:30a      Directory C:\DATA\WPDATA\*.*
Document size:  0      Free:  20807680      Used:  0      Files:  4

. CURRENT <DIR>                    PARENT    <DIR>
POST01 .   <DIR>   28-11-89 12:41p   POST02 .    <DIR>    28-11-89 12:45p
POST03 .   <DIR>   28-11-89 12:47p   POST04 .    <DIR>    28-11-89 12:48p


New directory = C:\DATA\WPDATA
```

```
30-01-90  09:30a      Directory C:\DATA\WPDATA\POST02\*.*
Document size:  0      Free:  20807680      Used:  9915      Files:  9

   CURRENT <DIR>                    ..    PARENT  <DIR>
ABC        .LET   1299   28-11-89 08:30a   APPEND   .LET    796   19-12-89 15:20p
DESIGNER .LET    964   28-11-89 09:30a   LETTER12 .LET   1368   28-11-89 11:21a
MASTER    .LET   1283   20-12-89 09:42a   MERGE    .LET    705   19-12-89 10:22a
PRIMARY  .LET   1335   19-12-89 09:55a   ROLES     .LET   1062   19-12-89 14:30p
TRAIN     .LET   1112   20-12-89 08.40a




1 Retrieve;  2 Delete;  3 Move/Rename;  4 Print;  5 Short/Long Display;
6 Look;  7 Other Directory;  8 Copy;  9 Find;  N Name Search: 6
```

❶ Press **7**. Type the name of the new directory you want to move to (for example C\DATA\ WPDATA\POST02). Then press **Enter** twice.

or
Use the cursor keys to highlight POST02. Then press **7** and **Enter** twice.

● You are now in the POST02 directory.

COPY

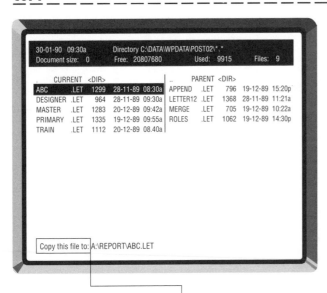

```
30-01-90  09:30a      Directory C:\DATA\WPDATA\POST02\*.*
Document size:  0      Free:  20807680      Used:  9915      Files:  9

   CURRENT <DIR>                    ..    PARENT  <DIR>
ABC        .LET   1299   28-11-89 08:30a   APPEND   .LET    796   19-12-89 15:20p
DESIGNER .LET    964   28-11-89 09:30a   LETTER12 .LET   1368   28-11-89 11:21a
MASTER    .LET   1283   20-12-89 09:42a   MERGE    .LET    705   19-12-89 10:22a
PRIMARY  .LET   1335   19-12-89 09:55a   ROLES     .LET   1062   19-12-89 14:30p
TRAIN     .LET   1112   20-12-89 08.40a




Copy this file to:  A:\REPORT\ABC.LET
```

Copying to the current directory

To copy a file within the current directory its name must be changed. For example, to copy ABC.DOC, type after the prompt: **ABC.COP** and then press **Enter**.

The new file name will not appear immediately. Use the cursor keys to highlight *"Current <DIR>"* and then press **Enter** twice to update the listing.

Copying to another drive and/or directory

Type the new drive and directory. For example, to copy ABC.LET to drive A, REPORT directory, type after the prompt: **A:\REPORT\ABC.LET** and press **Enter**. The file is now copied to the **A:\REPORT** directory.

❶ Use the cursor control keys to highlight the file to be copied.

❷ Press **8** and the prompt:*"Copy this file to:"* appears.

INTRODUCTION   DELETE/
                      MOVE OR
                      RENAME/
                      PRINT/LOOK

OTHER
DIRECTORY/
COPY/NAME
SEARCH

HELP

PULL
DOWN
MENUS

CREATE
AND
EDIT A
DOCUMENT

MOVE, COPY,
DELETE, AND
RESTORE
TEXT

FORMAT
YOUR
DOCUMENTS

CHECK
YOUR
DOCUMENTS

PRINT
YOUR
DOCUMENTS

MANAGE
YOUR
DOCUMENTS

MERGE
YOUR
DOCUMENTS

NAME SEARCH

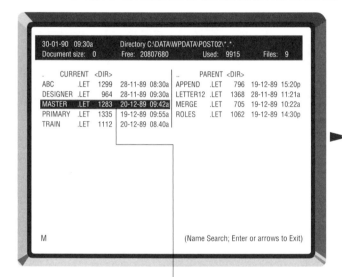

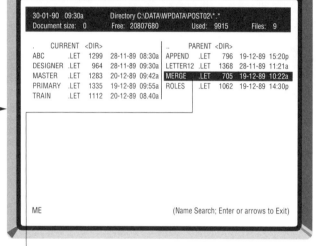

● The Name Search feature permits you to quickly find a document within your current directory.

❶ Press **N** to access Name Search.

❷ To find a file (for example, "*MERGE.LET*"), type **M** for the first letter in **M**ERGE. The file MASTER.LET is highlighted because its second letter (A) is alphabetically ahead of (E) in MFRGE.

❸ Type the second letter in M**E**RGE or **E**, and the "*MERGE.LET*" file is highlighted.

❹ Press **Enter** to end the search.

❺ For directories containing large numbers of files, continue typing in the letters of the file name you want in sequence until it is highlighted.

*Note: Press **Backspace** to revert to the previous letter.*

To cancel other directory/copy/ name search
Press **F1**.

PRIMARY FILE

This file contains the standard text of the letter and the merge commands to tell WordPerfect where to insert the customized information.

Note: This file does not have to use all the fields in the Secondary file.

December 19, 1989
{FIELD}1~
{FIELD}2~
{FIELD}3~, {FIELD}4~
{FIELD}5~

Dear {FIELD}6~:

On behalf of our bank, I would like to invite you to attend our Open House on January 3, 1990.

Coffee and donuts will be served, and our staff will be available to answer any questions you may have.

{Field}6~, I look forward to meeting you.

Yours truly,

B.A. Jones
Manager

MERGED FILE

This file contains documents containing the merged information from both the Primary and Secondary files.

Document 1

December 19, 1989

Mr. B. Wilson
1750 Victoria Park Ave.
Toronto, Ontario
M1K 5H3

Dear Mr. Wilson

On behalf of our bank, I would like to invite you to attend our Open House on January 3, 1990.

Coffee and donuts will be served, and our staff will be available to answer any questions you may have.

Mr. Wilson, I look forward to meeting you.

Yours truly,

B.A. Jones
Manager

INTRODUCTION

CREATING THE
PRIMARY
FILE

CREATING THE
SECONDARY
FILE

MERGING THE
PRIMARY AND
SECONDARY
FILES

HELP

PULL
DOWN
MENUS

CREATE
AND
EDIT A
DOCUMENT

MOVE, COPY,
DELETE, AND
RESTORE
TEXT

FORMAT
YOUR
DOCUMENTS

CHECK
YOUR
DOCUMENTS

PRINT
YOUR
DOCUMENTS

MANAGE
YOUR
DOCUMENTS

**MERGE
YOUR
DOCUMENTS**

SECONDARY FILE

This file contains the customized information (names, addresses, etc.) to go into each letter. Each group of information is called a record and contains the data for each separate customer.

The information in each **record** is broken down into different **fields**. For example, a customer's name may be in one field, the address in another, etc.

Record 1

Field 1	Name: Mr. B. Wilson
Field 2	Address: 1750 Victoria Park Ave.
Field 3	City: Toronto
Field 4	Province: Ontario
Field 5	Postal: M1K 5H3
Field 6	Salutation: Mr. Wilson

Record 2

Field 1	Name: Mr. G. Johnston
Field 2	Address:15 Brookbanks Drive
Field 3	City: North York
Field 4	Province: Ontario
Field 5	Postal: M5V 3H2
Field 6	Salutation: Mr. Johnston

Record 3

Field 1	Name: Ms. E. Allister
Field 2	Address: 12 Willow Avenue
Field 3	City: North York
Field 4	Province: Ontario
Field 5	Postal: M6V 2R4
Field 6	Salutation: Ms. Allister

When creating the Secondary file, each field **must** contain the same information in every record.

For example, if the first field of one record contains the customer name, the first field of **every** record must contain the customer name.

Note: The Secondary file must contain all the fields used in the Primary file.

Document 2

December 19, 1989

Mr. G. Johnston
15 Brookbanks Drive
North York, Ontario
M5V 3H2

Dear Mr. Johnston

On behalf of our bank, I would like to invite you
to attend our Open House on January 3, 1990.

Coffee and donuts will be served, and our staff will be
available to answer any questions you may have.

Mr. Johnston, I look forward to meeting you.

Yours truly,

B.A. Jones
Manager

Document 3

December 19, 1989

Ms. E. Allister
12 Willow Avenue
North York, Ontario
M6V 2R4

Dear Ms. Allister

On behalf of our bank, I would like to invite you
to attend our Open House on January 3, 1990.

Coffee and donuts will be served, and our staff will be
available to answer any questions you may have.

Ms. Allister, I look forward to meeting you.

Yours truly,

B.A. Jones
Manager

CREATING THE PRIMARY FILE

Before creating the file, decide on how the information will be split into different fields. For example, the entire address may be treated as one field, or it may be broken down into *"address"*, *"city"*, *"province"*, and *"postal"* (this may be of benefit later on if only parts of the address are required in a merge).

In this example, the information is broken down as follows:

Field 1	Name
Field 2	Address
Field 3	City
Field 4	Province
Field 5	Postal
Field 6	Salutation

Note: After deciding on the fields, keep a record of this information on paper to keep track of them for creating the Secondary file.

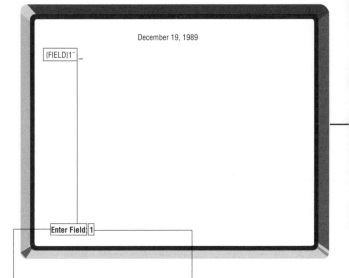

Date

❶ Type the date and press **Enter** to move the cursor to the location for placing Field 1.

Field 1 – Name

❷ To insert *Field 1*, press **Shift-F9** and type **F**. The prompt *"Enter Field:"* appears on the screen.

❸ Type **1** to identify Field 1 and press **Enter**. *"{FIELD}1~"* appears on screen.

❹ Press **Enter** to move to the next line.

HELP

PULL DOWN MENUS

CREATE AND EDIT A DOCUMENT

MOVE, COPY, DELETE, AND RESTORE TEXT

FORMAT YOUR DOCUMENTS

CHECK YOUR DOCUMENTS

PRINT YOUR DOCUMENTS

MANAGE YOUR DOCUMENTS

MERGE YOUR DOCUMENTS

```
                    December 19, 1989

{FIELD}1~
{FIELD}2~
{FIELD}3~, {FIELD}4~
{FIELD}5~ _




                                        Doc 1  Pg 1  Ln 2.33"  Pos 1.2"
```

```
                    December 19, 1989

{FIELD}1~
{FIELD}2~
{FIELD}3~, {FIELD}4~
{FIELD}5~

Dear  {FIELD}6~:

    On behalf of our bank, I would like to invite you
to attend our Open House on January 3, 1990.

    Coffee and donuts will be served, and our staff will be
available to answer any questions you may have.

{FIELD}6~, I look forward to meeting you.

                        Yours truly,

                        B.A. Jones
                        Manager_

                                        Doc 1  Pg 1  Ln 4.67"  Pos 5.7"
```

Field 2 – Address

❶ To insert Field 2, press **Shift-F9** and type **F**. Then type **2** to identify Field 2 and press **Enter**. *"{FIELD}2~"* appears on screen.

❷ Press **Enter** to move to the next line.

Fields 3 and 4 – City and Province

❸ To insert both these fields on the same line, press **Shift-F9** and type **F**. Then Type **3** and press **Enter**. *"{FIELD}3~"* appears on screen.

Next type a comma followed by a space. Press **Shift-F9** and type **F**. Then type **4** and press **Enter**. *"{FIELD}4~"* appears on screen.

❹ Press **Enter** to move to the next line.

Field 5 – Postal Code

❺ To insert Field 5 press **Shift-F9** and type **F**. Type **5** to identify field 5 and press **Enter**. *"{FIELD}5~"* appears on screen.

❻ Press **Enter** twice to move to the salutation line.

Field 6 – Salutation

❶ Type the word **Dear** followed by a space and then insert Field 6 by pressing **Shift-F9** and type **F**. Type **6** to identify Field 6 and press **Enter**. *"{FIELD}6~"* appears on the screen.

❷ Next type the colon (:) after *"{FIELD}6~"*.

❸ Continue typing the rest of the letter.

Note: If any of the fields must be used again, follow this procedure:

*Press **Shift-F9**, Type **F**, type the original field number, and press **Enter** (fields may be used as often as necessary in the Primary file).*

Spellcheck and save the document

Spellcheck the document using **Ctrl-F2**. It is more efficient to spellcheck the Primary file than the merged file. This is because the Merged file contains many names and addresses that slow down the process).

Press **F7** to save the document and clear the screen.

CREATING THE SECONDARY FILE

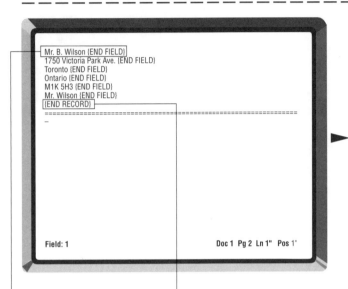

```
Mr. B. Wilson {END FIELD}
1750 Victoria Park Ave. {END FIELD}
Toronto {END FIELD}
Ontario {END FIELD}
M1K 5H3 {END FIELD}
Mr. Wilson {END FIELD}
{END RECORD}
================================================
_
```

Field: 1   Doc 1 Pg 2 Ln 1" Pos 1"

```
Mr. B. Wilson {END FIELD}
1750 Victoria Park Ave. {END FIELD}
Toronto {END FIELD}
Ontario {END FIELD}
M1K 5H3 {END FIELD}
Mr. Wilson {END FIELD}
{END RECORD}
================================================
Mr. G. Johnston {END FIELD}
15 Brookbanks Drive {END FIELD}
North York {END FIELD}
Ontario {END FIELD}
M5V 3H2 {END FIELD}
Mr. Johnston {END FIELD}
{END RECORD}
================================================
Ms. E. Allister {END FIELD}
12 Willow Ave. {END FIELD}
North York {END FIELD}
Ontario {END FIELD}
M6V 2R4 {END FIELD}
```

Field: 3   Doc 1 Pg 3 Ln 1" Pos 1"

Field 1 - Name

❶ Type the first customer's name (this is the first piece of Field 1 information).

❷ Press **F9** to insert the code *"{END FIELD}"* (this identifies the end of the first customer's name and moves the cursor to the next line).

Fields 2 to 5

❸ Follow steps **1** and **2** for each of the other fields of data.

Ending the first record

❹ After pressing **F9** to complete the last field, press **Shift-F9** and then **2** to tell WordPerfect that this is the end of the record. *"{END RECORD}"* appears on the screen.

Typing in remaining records

❺ Follow steps **1** to **4** until all records have been typed.

❻ When finished, press **F7** to save the file and clear the screen.

Note: If a particular field is empty in a record, still include the {END FIELD} code to ensure that the correct field numbering is maintained in that record.

INTRODUCTION   CREATING THE
                PRIMARY
                FILE

**CREATING THE
SECONDARY
FILE**

**MERGING THE
PRIMARY AND
SECONDARY
FILES**

HELP

PULL
DOWN
MENUS

CREATE
AND
EDIT A
DOCUMENT

MOVE, COPY,
DELETE, AND
RESTORE
TEXT

FORMAT
YOUR
DOCUMENTS

CHECK
YOUR
DOCUMENTS

PRINT
YOUR
DOCUMENTS

MANAGE
YOUR
DOCUMENTS

**MERGE
YOUR
DOCUMENTS**

MERGING THE PRIMARY AND SECONDARY FILES

```
1 Merge; 2 Sort; 3 Convert Old Merge Codes: 0
```

```
                              December 19, 1989

Ms. E. Allister
12 Willow Ave.
North York, Ontario
M6V 2R4

Dear Ms. Allister:

    On behalf of our bank, I would like to invite you
to attend our Open House on January 3, 1990.

    Coffee and donuts will be served, and our staff will be
available to answer any questions you may have.

    Ms. Allister, I look forward to meeting you.

                         Yours truly,

                         B.A. Jones
                         Manager_

                              Doc 1 Pg 3 Ln 4.67" Pos 5.7"
```

● Make sure the typing area is empty before beginning step **1**.

❶ Press **Ctrl-F9** and the prompt *"1 Merge; 2 Sort; 3 Convert Old Merge Codes: 0"* appears.

❷ Type **1** to select Merge.

❸ Type the name of the Primary file and press **Enter**. See note below.

❹ Type the name of the Secondary file and press **Enter**.

Note: To convert WordPerfect 5.0 Primary and Secondary Merge files to the 5.1 format, press 3.

● The merged document appears on screen. Always scroll through and/or view the final, merged document before printing to ensure no problems occurred.

Note: After printing the Merged document, the Merged file can be erased from the hard disk to save space (as long as the Primary and Secondary files are retained).

CREATING ENVELOPES FOR A MERGE

To create envelopes for a merge (if your printer can handle envelopes), follow these steps:

❶ In an empty typing area, press **Shift-F8** and select **Option 2, Page**

❷ Choose **Option 5, Margins** and set the top margin to 2" and the bottom margin to .5". **Choose Option 7** Paper Size/Type. Select the Envelope form. Press **Enter** to return to the main formatting menu.

❸ Select **Option 1, Line**, and choose **Option 7, Margins**. Set the left margin at 3.5". When finished, press **F7** to return to the typing area.

❹ Type the field names in the typing area, beginning at the left margin. For example:

{Field}1~
{Field}2~
{Field}3~, {Field}4~
{Field}5~

❺ Save the file and clear the screen.

❻ To merge this new primary file with the existing secondary file, press **Ctrl-F9**, choose **Option 1, Merge**, type the name of the new Primary file and press **Enter**. Then type the name of the Secondary file and press **Enter**.

Index